WAR, CONFLICT AND PLAY

Debating Play Series

Series Editor: Tina Bruce, Honorary Visiting Professor at University of Surrey, Roehampton

The intention behind the 'Debating Play' series is to encourage readers to reflect on their practices so that they are in a position to offer high quality play opportunities to children. The series will help those working with young children and their families, in diverse ways and contexts, to think about how to cultivate early childhood play with rich learning potential.

The 'Debating Play' series examines cultural myths and taboos. It considers matters of human rights and progress towards inclusion in the right to play for children with complex needs. It looks at time-honoured practices and argues for the removal of constraints on emergent play. It challenges readers to be committed to promoting play opportunities for children traumatized by war, flight, violence and separation from loved ones. The series draws upon crucial contemporary research which demonstrates how children in different parts of the world develop their own play culture in ways which help them make sense of their lives.

Published and forthcoming titles

Forbes: *Beginning to Play*
Holland: *We Don't Play With Guns Here*
Hyder: *War, Conflict and Play*
Kalliala: *Play Culture in a Changing World*
Manning-Morton and Thorp: *Key Times for Play*
Orr: *My Right to Play: A Child with Complex Needs*

CONTENTS

Series editor's preface   vii
Acknowledgements   ix

Introduction   1

1   **Children and development: the importance
    of play**   5

2   **Being a refugee: the loss of play**   24

3   **The impact of war, conflict and violence on young
    children: the consequences for play**   41

4   **What works: first principles to promote play**   60

5   **Lessons from practice: the role
    of play**   77

6   **War and violence in the wider world: issues
    affecting play**   90

7   **Conclusion: play as a child's right**   100

Bibliography   102
Index   108

SERIES EDITOR'S PREFACE

I was delighted when Tina Hyder agreed to write this book. She has, through her work with Save the Children, developed great expertise and understanding of the issues for children and families who are living through war and conflict, and those who become refugees or asylum seekers. She has a very measured approach to these deeply distressing situations, and helps the reader to get on the inside of what this means to children and families in ways which allow reflection and quietly thought through action, so that feelings do not run so high that they constrain what can be achieved.

The book is holistic in its approach, but it gives a major focus to the importance of play for children living through war, or as refugees, thus keeping the spirit and emphasis of the 'Debating Play' Series. Play is as important, if not more important than ordinarily for children living such extraordinary lives. Tina Hyder sets the scene for the reader, addressing questions such as who is a refugee, why refugees leave their home, what happens to families when they arrive in the UK, and the problems that relate to ensuring the children have opportunities for play.

Children and families are influenced by their experiences of war and becoming refugees in ways which affect their relationship with their parents, carers and their general development. Tina Hyder shows how play has a restorative impact on development and relationships. Good early years practice, emphasising the importance of play, are central in developing this. She outlines some of the theories of play which are helpful in taking early years practice forward. She gives case studies which demonstrate how, using various approaches which bring healing through play, children affected by the direct and indirect experience of violence can be helped to develop in positive ways.

This book embraces the principles of diversity and inclusion and consequently it will give readers a framework for play which will benefit all children, but it will give particular help to practitioners supporting children affected by conflict and war.

Professor Tina Bruce
Series Editor

ACKNOWLEDGEMENTS

There are many children, families and colleagues who have inspired and informed this book. I would particularly like to mention the children, families and staff of Salusbury World; Lois Mutesi; Babette Brown, and the early years service in Islington.

I would also like to say a very heartfelt thank you to Tina Bruce for her support and encouragement throughout. This book really would not have been possible without her.

Thanks also to my former colleagues at London Metropolitan University; and also colleagues, past and present, at Save the Children.

And, as always, thank you to Charles and Yasmin.

Tina Hyder
July 2004

INTRODUCTION

This book is about the many ways play can make a positive difference in the lives of an extraordinary group of children – the young refugees and asylum-seekers from many parts of the world who are increasingly part of our social fabric.

Every morning or evening in our homes, we listen to news about war or civil unrest; these events, with their often devastating impact on children as well as adults, are occurring in parts of the world that seem remote – and yet are closer than we think.

Some of you will have had direct experience of such events, but for many of us the plight of those affected by conflict is something we observe from afar. However, as globalization impacts on all aspects of our lives, war and conflict in what may appear to be far-flung parts of the world are coming to affect all of us closer to home. The wars that we see unfold in front of us on our television screens translate into the presence of real families and children in our early years settings and schools.

This book aims to examine the crucial importance of play for children's development. It then looks at the experience of being a refugee, and the implications of war and conflict for young children's development. It goes on to consider how best we can support, through play, the young children for whom we care.

Families with children seeking a safe haven have of course been coming to the UK for many years, and some readers of this book will already be familiar with the numerous issues that arise from working with refugee and asylum-seeking families; the book aims to help you reflect on your experiences.

For others, including those readers who are training to work with young children and families, involvement in early years settings with asylum-seeking and refugee children may be new, and you may be looking for insights to support your practice.

Finally, the book aims to provide an additional perspective to enable you to see beyond the frequent 'scare story' headlines and stereotypes presented in newspapers, and understand that they do not always give the full picture.

Asylum and the response of governments and their peoples to the numbers of refugees in today's world are controversial issues, politically, economically and socially. It is beyond the scope of this book to comment on wider political issues in any detail. But it does take as its starting point the firm commitment to the rights of all children which was first articulated by Eglantyne Jebb, the founder of Save the Children, precisely as a specific response to the suffering of children affected by war and conflict in Europe in the early part of the last century.

Jebb founded Save the Children in 1919, and some of the first children she helped were the children of the 'enemy'. At the end of the First World War there were severe food shortages in cities such as Berlin and Vienna, and reports that 6-year-olds were so malnourished that they looked like 2-year-olds. An eye-witness account from 1919 by Dr Hector Munro invoked the following picture:

> Conditions were indeed terrible. Children were actually dying in the street. I saw in the Allgemeine Krankenhaus 38 women who were suffering spontaneous fracture of the hips, their bones having lost all solidity. The children's bones were like rubber. Tuberculosis was terribly rife. Clothing was utterly lacking. Children were wrapped in paper, and in the hospitals there was nothing but paper bandages.
>
> (Save the Children 2003)

Jebb, along with her sister, Dorothy Buxton, sought to raise public awareness of the plight of these children, and elicit sympathy and support for the suffering inhabitants of the vanquished nations, initially by producing leaflets highlighting the impact of famine in Europe. Jebb was even arrested in 1919 in Trafalgar Square for distributing copies of a pamphlet entitled 'A Starving Baby'.

Undeterred, the sisters went on to found Save the Children, initially as a temporary organization working to raise money for children's organizations all over war-torn Europe – and operating firmly according to the children's rights principles set out by Jebb: that children should not be made to suffer for the actions of adults. This rights-based approach continues to underpin the work of Save the Children today, as children globally face the consequences of war and civil conflict. The organization works in accordance with Jebb's belief that humanity has a collective responsibility to provide for children, whatever the nature of political conflict.

This focus on the rights of children, innovative as it was in the early part of the twentieth century, came to be of increasing importance to Jebb, and to her fledgling Save the Children organization:

> I believe we should claim certain Rights for the children and labour for their universal recognition, so that everybody – not merely the small number of people who are in a position to contribute to relief funds, but everybody who in any way comes into contact with children, that is to say the vast majority of mankind – may be in a position to help forward the movement.

This prototype of the *Declaration of the Rights of the Child* was adopted and promoted by the International Save the Children Union in 1923, and within a year was adopted by the League of Nations and achieved lasting international significance.

The present *United Nations Convention on the Rights of the Child* (*UNCRC*), adopted in 1989, is derived from Eglantyne Jebb's early statements (Save the Children 2003). It sets out a framework for governments to recognize and actively pursue, through policy and legislation, the rights of all children. The UK government ratified the convention in 1991.

It is important to note the distinction between the concept of children having 'needs' as opposed to 'rights'. On the one hand, the 'needs' of one group are often defined by another more powerful group, and meeting 'needs' can be an optional action by those who are in a more powerful position – both to define a need and then to decide whether or not to meet it. On the other hand, the concept of 'rights' suggests a set of legal imperatives or entitlements that governments and other institutions have a duty in law to uphold. In this formulation, and as the culmination of the process initiated by Jebb, children are now seen to have internationally recognized human rights. This is a shift from the idea that children are the property of their parents – instead, the state has a duty to recognize the child as an *individual*, and to support families to provide the best possible start for their children.

The fundamental principles of the *UNCRC*, all of which work towards enhancing children's development, are:

- non-discrimination (all rights apply to all children);
- best interests (all decisions, actions and policies should take into account their impact on children);

- participation (children have a right to express opinions on matters that affect them);
- survival and development.

The rights set out in the *UNCRC* cover almost every aspect of children's lives. The *Convention* specifically requires governments to take into account the rights of refugee and asylum-seeking children. The relevant section is Article 22, setting obligations for governments to offer protection to children seeking refugee status and to ensure that those children enjoy all the other rights set out in the *Convention*.

In addition, the *Convention* also sets out the child's right to play. Article 31 states that 'all children have a fundamental right to leisure, play and recreation' (United Nations 1989).

This book will bring together theories of children's play with information about the impact of war and conflict on young children – with the aim of helping practitioners put Article 31 into practice for refugee and asylum-seeking children. It also provides some practical information about the processes and context of being a refugee in the UK today. And it will offer examples of the ways early years services can best respond to and support asylum-seeking and refugee children and families. It will describe practical, play-based activities that practitioners can undertake with young children. Finally, the underpinning argument of this book is that *play is a healing experience for young children affected by war and conflict*. Moreover, this assertion is not just about play in isolation, as a process in which the individual child takes part. It is also about play as a part of the social fabric of a community and as a dynamic exchange between the child and their world. Play can return to the children of conflict their lost childhoods.

Terminology

The terms 'asylum-seeker' and 'refugee' have precise and distinct legal meanings. An asylum-seeker is waiting to be recognized as a refugee – that is, as someone with a well-founded fear of persecution under international law (see p. 26 ff. for a fuller explanation). However, the terms are not always used consistently in the media and elsewhere. In this book the term 'refugee' is used to encompass both states, unless specifically referring to conditions affecting one group or the other.

The terms 'war', 'conflict' and 'violence' refer to a vast range of military and political crises. In many cases these categories cannot be disentangled. For the purposes of this book what is meant are situations of civil, political and social upheaval characterized by armed violence whether between or within nations.

1

CHILDREN AND DEVELOPMENT: THE IMPORTANCE OF PLAY

> When we take care of children, we are also helping the human species
> find the truth and understand the world.
>
> (Gopnik *et al*. 1999: 211)

This chapter begins by looking at what elements need to be in place to ensure that children develop to their full potential and have opportunities to explore and extend all their capacities and capabilities. It will further explore the generalized impact on children's development of social breakdown because of war and conflict – looking in detail at the developmental processes of early childhood, and noting what happens when that progress is interrupted.

The major theories of play will be outlined, with the emphasis here on play not only as a necessary feature of childhood and essential component of development, but also as a means to regain 'lost childhoods'.

The context for development

The starting point is an examination and exploration of the ideal conditions for development. This rests on the simple question: What do children need in order to develop?

What springs to mind if you pause for a moment to reflect on this? Clearly there are some basic components: love, security, food, shelter, a family and community, opportunities for play, self-expression and interaction, healthcare and other welfare support, and education in its broadest sense. These are just some of the elements that can contribute towards a positive early childhood. Research into child development does indeed reveal that the achievement of full potential rests on the basic human requirements of food, shelter, protection, care and affection being met by children's caregivers.

At the same time, opportunities to explore the physical environment, interaction with others and induction into the rituals and norms of their communities, through the structure of language, relationships, song, art and story, are also essential for all children.

It is through considering all these elements that we begin to appreciate the full meaning of child development – that is, the holistic growth and maturation of a child's emotional, social, physical and intellectual capacities, equipping them to participate in their communities and cultures.

From their earliest days, children are also developing individual skills, competencies and interests that form the foundation for all that follows. What has been described above should not be an exceptional experience for some children but is the right of *all* children.

In peaceful, affluent societies it can be very easy to take these building blocks for development for granted. But even in communities that are relatively materially well off all these components are not always in place for children. To give just one example, the rates of child abuse in the UK point to the fact that, even within a society that is relatively wealthy, this material security alone does not guarantee a positive childhood. Nevertheless, material and practical support provides a framework within which it is easier to operate a functioning community and family network, in which positive child development can take place.

How war affects communities

In countries and communities where political, social and economic instability leads to civil conflict, or when there is war between countries, the material aspects of a community, its institutions and services, are disrupted and weakened. This in turn impacts on the abilities of families and individuals always to maintain the emotional focus on growing children, as attention instead has to be placed on securing food, healthcare and so on.

It is sometimes easy to see the impact of war just in terms of loss of life, injury and damage to the concrete environment, whether this is in the destruction of buildings or the loss of services such as power and water supplies. However, it is important to acknowledge that the impact of the chaos caused to the social fabric of families and communities can be as damaging for the development of the child as any concrete impact. For young children, it is the fact that their carers are perhaps emotionally and physically exhausted, and unable to call on the usual support normally available at times of family crisis, which will have a profound impact.

From this perspective of social as well as physical damage, we will begin to build the case for the importance of play as a restorative and healing experience for young children. This is not just because play in itself is a formative experience for the individual child, but also because play is rooted in the experience and representation of events and objects within a family and a community.

It is important to consider the everyday life of the developing child in order to really appreciate and understand the ways that war, conflict and violence severely undermine and distort childhoods. Apart from the obvious and direct material impact of violence in a community and the subsequent dangers of injury and death, there are other, less visible, impacts on children.

These less visible pressures on children and children's lives are often the consequence of the destruction of the social networks and mores that bind a community. This may be hard to imagine for those of us who have never lived in such circumstances, as there is much that we take for granted about acceptable behaviours in our daily lives.

In most communities there are unspoken and codified norms of behaviour and interaction that mediate all our daily experiences. These norms are underpinned by tradition and custom, and are further reinforced by stable political and social structures. Behavioural norms are, day in and day out, reflected back in popular culture, through television or in newspapers and magazines. These norms are also transmitted to children in other ways – for instance, through stories and religious and social practices.

When those norms are violated – for example in the UK today when parents are neglectful or when partners are abusive – such behaviours are condemned, and this process of social reinforcement (through civil and social structures, whether they are religious, political or social) can be seen in all communities worldwide.

What is acceptable and what is not acceptable will clearly vary over time and place. Nevertheless, although there are exceptions, it can be argued that there are universal norms, shared by most human communities. These include sanctions against killing, taboos against incest, respect for elders in a community and responsibility for the young.

As already noted, one of the less obvious impacts of war, civil conflict and continual violence in a community is the erosion of social and behavioural norms. The stress of having to cope with and adapt to ongoing violence causes people to behave and react in extreme ways. For some people, a coping mechanism will be to flout normally agreed and acceptable forms of behaviour in an effort to regain control over an uncontrollable situation, or just because there is nothing to stop them. An alternative means of coping might be the attempt to regain control by exerting sway over those who have even less power.

This is why, again and again, one of the reported results of ongoing conflict, whether due to war or civil conflict, is that rates of violence towards women and children increase. This is the case within all communities, including those that are under attack and those that are the aggressors.

This may be manifest in increased levels of child rape and child abuse. The normal sanctions and protective mechanisms that maintain order in societies are removed at times of social upheaval, and vulnerable populations are therefore made even more vulnerable at times of crisis.

Bronfenbrenner's model of 'ecological development' (1979) sets this out in a particularly clear way – describing four layers or concentric circles of society all of which impact on the child, and within which the child is an active agent (although it was only some time later that Bronfenbrenner acknowledged the agency of the child).

These layers start with the child in the centre surrounded by the immediate and extended family. Next there is the direct community, with friends and neighbours. Surrounding this are institutions such as schools or health services, religious and other leaders, and at the outside are the larger national institutions and services, government and media, all reinforcing values and beliefs.

Children are active participants in this model, caught in a dynamic process where their lives are shaped by all the influences around them and they in turn have an impact. Therefore, while it is important to see how unusual and traumatic events affect the individual directly, it is also important to realize that much of the impact on the individual is due to the dismantling of wider relationships, social networks and institutions. This chapter will go on to bring together thinking about individual development against the context of wider social, political and cultural connections, and look at the vital role of play in development and in healing.

How children develop

There are increasing strides being made in the field of child development. More is now known about the importance of the early years of life, and how later patterns of behaviour are shaped by early experiences, than ever before. This is demonstrated particularly by research in the last ten years into the development of the brain in infancy. We will explore this research later in the chapter.

Child development is a continuous process, but there are distinct phases. The period from birth to the age of 3 sees children's evolving capacities at their most active. Children are learning to walk and talk, to form relationships and to become part of a family and community. The natural world also provides an area of enormous fascination.

The safety to explore and to overcome challenges is one of the key features of this point in life – particularly through play. While this may be taken for granted, when safety and security do not surround a child and family the opportunities for children to test and extend their evolving capacities are not available, and this has a negative impact on the child's development. Birth to 3, while being a key period of development, is a time when children are particularly vulnerable in terms of survival and damage if conditions are not conducive (Molteno 1996).

From 3 onwards children lay claim to their wishes for independence and autonomy versus their roles and responsibilities in relation to others. Children are testing their physical abilities and experimenting with their physical and social environments. Linguistic development is rapid at this stage. Friendships, treasured objects and interests are all part of the assertion of self. The adult and natural worlds provide endless opportunities for investigation and learning – and if this learning is supported and encouraged, children develop and gain confidence in themselves and their competencies.

Taking this as a snapshot of the process of child development, the academic focus in the past has typically been on the debate between those convinced about the influence of genetic inheritance versus those emphasizing environmental factors (nature vs. nurture). Evidence now points to an interactionist perspective as offering the most informed and accurate framework for child development at this point. This means that the biological characteristics of a child are in constant interplay with the child's environment. One shapes and responds to the other.

An acknowledgement therefore of the complexity of the child's social and environmental systems, as demonstrated in Bronfenbrenner's model of ecological development, referred to above, is essential. This is because children develop through social interactions and social structures – all of which have an important influence on the child's overall individual development.

Early brain development

In the past, it was believed that the structure of the brain was genetically predetermined and largely in place before birth. Scientists were not aware of the enormous and formative impact of an infant's first experiences.

Research in infant neuroscience (see Gopnik *et al.* 1999) reveals that from birth, and before, the infant's brain is full of cells that trigger in response to their interactions and experiences of the world.

The nerve cells in the brain are called neurons, and they are in place before birth. At the time of birth infants have approximately a thousand billion brain cells. Each neuron has a long fibre (axon) that sends information in the form of electrical impulses to other cells. Information is also received from other cells through short fibres (dendrites).

At birth, the neurons are not connected. As children grow and an increasing amount of information is received in the brain, the dendrites branch out, forming tree-like structures as they receive signals from many neurons. Early brain development is about the formation and reinforcement of such connections. The point at which neurons connect and exchange information is called the *synapse*: 'Connections among neurons are formed as the growing child experiences the surrounding world and forms attachments to parents, family members, and other caregivers' (Shore 1997: 17). Therefore, an infant's early experiences create neural activity and subsequent neural connections, that can be in place for life (Gopnik *et al.* 1999).

New technologies, such as MRI (magnetic resonance imaging – showing the brain structure) and PET (positron emission tomography – measuring brain activity) scans and other brain imaging technologies have revealed that the brain, from before birth and onwards, is affected by environmental factors. And it is during the first three years of life that the majority of developmental neural and synaptic activity takes place – setting out the networks for later life.

From birth onwards there is a rapid and enormous growth in synaptic activity that peaks at about the age of 3. At 3 children have more neural pathways than adults, and children's brains are two and a half times more active that the brains of adults (Shore 1997: 21). This synaptic density remains in place until about the age of 10, when unused synaptic connections fall away.

Clearly, these research findings indicate that early experiences are even more important than once believed. The neural pathways that become established are those that are in repeated use. In this way, early experiences have a decisive impact on how the brain becomes wired. (Gopnik *et al.* 1999). What this means is that early experiences have an overall effect on children's abilities to relate to others and to the external world, to learn, to express their feelings and to take forward their overall development.

Of enormous importance appears to be the fact that an infant's early experiences are mediated by their primary caregiver. What this means is that the quality of the infant-carer relationship is of crucial significance for early brain development. Therefore, as Shore (1997: 26) notes: 'Neuroscientists are finding that a strong, secure attachment to a nurturing caregiver can have a protective biological function, helping a child withstand (and indeed, learn from) the ordinary stresses of daily life. There is no single "right" way to create this capacity; warm, responsive care can take many forms'.

It is also important to bear in mind that the brain can change in response to new stimuli, so later experiences will also have an impact. There are also critical periods in children's developmental progress that are crucial for certain parts of brain functioning. For instance, those areas of the brain that regulate stress (the limbic system) are wired early in life, perhaps before the age of 6 months (Shore 1997).

Negative experiences such as maternal depression can also impact on the infant. It has been demonstrated, while not true in all cases, that maternal depression can adversely affect healthy brain development, particularly affecting the area of the brain associated with emotions. There are other risk factors such as alcohol and drug abuse that can be seen to have a long-lasting effect on the developing child and are now demonstrated to influence cognitive functioning in a negative way.

The predictability of the physical environment, access to health services, family stress and continuity of care are all now seen to have not just an emotional but also a biological impact on the young child. It is also important to note that researchers such as Greenspan and Wider, 1997 cited in Shore 1997, believe that interventions can mediate and compensate for negative early experiences.

Research (see Shore 1997; Gopnik *et al.* 1999) also makes a link between early brain development and stress and the development of the endocrine and immune systems. This means that if a child is exposed to continual stress and trauma when an infant, and the caregivers are unable to mitigate this impact, the child will become over-sensitized to stress and will be on constant guard, responding to threats and stresses even when such threats are not great.

It is important to pause for a moment here and consider in more detail what we mean by 'stress' in relation to very young infants. When we are adults, stressful situations are those when we feel we have lost control, or when we are doing something for the first time.

Often what is helpful is that there is some part of the experience that we are familiar with, that we can build on for reassurance. For instance, if we are taking an examination, previous experience of tests and examinations will help us determine what strategies we need to put in place to reduce stress.

From the perspective of a very young infant, the world is full of new experiences. This is why the routines and connections established in the early days between the infant and the caregiver are so important. The smallest interactions, whether in response to crying and being held, being fed or changed, or tone of voice, are potentially life-changing events for an infant, especially if the quality of that inter-action is harsh or uncaring, or undertaken by adults whose own lives are disrupted and insecure.

Trauma and neglect will impact in other ways on the development of the young child. For instance, a child's ability to form secure attachments will be influenced by the quality of the caregiving that they have had themselves.

It is also the case that the security of the attachment experienced by young children will affect their capacity to form relationships, to be empathetic and to express emotions and control behaviour. Gunnar's research, reported in Shore (1997: 28), suggests that 'babies who receive sensitive and nurturing care in their first year of life are less likely than other children to respond to minor stress'.

At the same time, under-stimulation, emotional neglect and social deprivation will also impact on children. Researchers in the USA (see Perry 1996) suggest that a combination of experiences may affect the brain's development. Stress or under-stimulation result in a lack of development of higher brain functions related to abstract thinking and behaviours; instead, lower brain functions associated with immediate survival responses are over-developed. This can lead to over-aggressive behaviours in response to ordinary occurrences, such as when someone raises their voice.

What then is the role of play in early brain development? Crucially, it would appear that play can actually shape and structure the brain, as researchers who have investigated the role of play in supporting synaptic development have found (see Jambor 2000).

Not all types of play do this; the function is most apparent in imaginative play characterized by engagement and interest. This play includes those fantasies and dramas that children initiate themselves and then choose to pursue and elaborate. It has elements of repetition and is fun. It activates and encourages neural pathways, and because it is often replayed, it promotes memory skills.

In conclusion, the current debate regarding brain development has highlighted the importance of the first three years of life. Nevertheless, researchers (e.g. Meade 2003) are now exploring the perception that, notwithstanding the importance of these first three years for children's development, later childhood and adulthood also provide opportunities for learning and development. Consequently, interventions such as daycare and early years services can be seen to be of benefit for children who have not necessarily had the best start.

The implications of this for those children and communities affected by war, conflict and violence are serious. Given what may be a crisis situation in early infancy, if children are to reach their full potential they need opportunities for secure and stable relationships with early caregivers in an environment that fosters the development of close and responsive relationships and opportunities for self-expression. Play can be a key way in which childhood can be restored.

The role of play in early childhood development

Play has been notoriously hard to define and research, and there are numerous theories about its purpose and form. This section will begin with a brief outline of the major theories of play. This will provide a backdrop upon which to reflect on what happens when opportunities to play are denied to young children whose lives have been disrupted by conflict. The section will then trace the impact of conflict on play as well as the role of play in restoring childhood.

The development of theories of play

> Ancient children played and, in a haphazard way, authors mentioned it. But no one wrote on play. Plato, who described how clumsy children were called donkeys, did not think that his philosopher-kings had to play.
>
> (Cohen 1993: 19)

Cohen's useful review of the academic literature on play notes the substantial absence of significant reflection on the subject until the nineteenth century, and recalls the words of Johan Huizinga, who in his pioneering text *Homo Ludens* (1949) criticized earlier writers on play: all their theories, he said, 'have one thing in common; they all start from the assumption that play must serve something that is not play, that it must serve some kind of biological purpose' (Cohen 1993: 19). According to Cohen, Huizinga goes on to assert that play is at the heart of all human development and is the basis for the development of human communities.

Huizinga's history of play reveals that interpretations of play are very much subject to their time. Trends in investigations into play tend to reflect wider cultural, political and scientific concerns. For instance, students of child development are familiar with the views of the philosopher Jean Jacques Rousseau (1712–78) who was perhaps one of the first people to argue the merits and importance of play. His views were very much a product of the Age of Enlightenment, and reflected concerns about the beginnings of technological development and investigation and man's autonomy in relation to nature and God.

In turn, Rousseau's views influenced other early educational thinkers such as Pestalozzi, Froebel, Montessori and others, all of whom saw play as a means by which children investigate and come to understand nature and the spiritual and material worlds, therefore emphasizing the notion of play with *purpose*.

Overall, these theories can be seen to resonate with the wider cultural and political themes of their times – and what this tells us is that writers are influenced not only by what has gone before but also by what is current. Hence, definitions of play, investigations into its function and purpose, and discussion of detail (e.g. the role of adults in guiding, shaping and extending play) have been and continue to be a source of debate, reflecting the wider debates of the age.

What is play?

> There is great difficulty in using the umbrella term 'play'. The focus needs to be refined so we can establish what is meant by this word. Many things called 'play' by those of us working with children are not so.
>
> (Bruce 1997: i)

It is useful to be aware of the main arguments and theories of play, as all of them have continuing influence on the way in which we conceptualize play today. This section will outline some of the major theories of play.

Theories of play can be said to fall into five main categories:

- play as a means of ridding the body of surplus energy or as an evolutionary phase;
- play as a means to understand the social world;
- play as a means of developing cognitive skills including language;
- play as means to come to terms with emotional and inner states;
- formal taxonomies of play.

What distinguishes play from other forms of human activity are its qualities of spontaneity and self-initiation. Across human cultures all children, in normal circumstances, have an intrinsic desire to play. The features of play include the symbolic use of objects, its pretend 'as if' nature, the construction of rules, and the fact that play is more often than not fun and risk-free, and does not have to have an end purpose.

Play enables children to explore the customs and roles of their direct community, to reflect upon their inner selves and their emotions, to encounter abstract thinking and to develop communication skills. Play is also often said to provide a vehicle for children to create meaning from their experiences (Bruce 1997).

We will now briefly review a range of theoretical perspectives on play. We can see that biologists, psychologists, anthropologists, sociologists and others have all attempted to define play from their particular theoretical standpoint.

Early theories tended to concentrate on global evolutionary explanations with a focus on the physical features of play. Later theorists have, in the main, focused on the internal, emotional functions of play. The cognitive role of play came to the fore in the mid-twentieth century, and has been a key feature of later approaches to play, influencing the development of services for young children.

More recently, there has been a consolidation of play theory, providing an overall holistic framework for child development within a social context. The significance of play within the developmental context has been increasingly recognized. Today, from a developmental perspective, we draw on a rich range of theories and ideas from a variety of academic disciplines, enabling us to value play as a vital way of being in early childhood.

Historical views of play

Herbert Spencer, in 1878, drew links between children's play and that of animals. He noted that play occurred because of excess energy. He also drew parallels between play and art, viewing art as a product of surplus energy after basic human needs had been met.

Spencer's ideas can be traced to those of Schiller (1845), who also saw play as a means for children to use up surplus energy. He suggested that it was because children did not have to work to survive, as adults did, that they therefore had amounts of energy that were not used. Play was important for adults too as it was linked to creativity and beauty. Other writers of the time thought that play in fact restored and did not deplete energy. These theories were known as 'recreation' or 'relaxation' theories.

Another interesting theory from the turn of the twentieth century was that of Hall (1908), who proposed that in play humans progress through all the stages of evolutionary development, and children's play is the evidence of this. For instance, the animal stage of human development is repeated in children's desire to climb and swing. Hall's 'recapitulation theory' rests on the notion that play provides an outlet for instinctive behaviours, and that play lessens instinctual urges.

Groos (1901), in *The Play of Man*, saw play as a preparation for adulthood, with children acting out and pretending to take on adult roles. He also began to elaborate the role of play as a means by which children develop consciousness. Later on Bruner (1983: 43 quoted in Bruce 1997: 31) extended this definition by describing play as 'preparation for the technical and social life that constitutes human culture'.

Similarly, Maria Montessori (1870–1952) placed importance on children learning about reality. She viewed pretend play as primitive and felt that children benefit from adult guidance to enable them to explore the properties of the real world through specially constructed play materials.

Behaviourist perspectives on play such as that of Skinner (1938) conceptualize play as a learnt response to a set of stimuli – for example, toys. Play was also seen as a set of problem-solving behaviours, because of its complex and investigative features.

More recently Bateson (1972), considered play as a means of developing children's communication skills. This theory is based on his observations of the shared 'scripts' that children create as they play together. Children will often talk about what a character will say and do, and then go on, in character, to act this out. This ability to reflect on communication, as Bateson observes, provides children with 'metacommunication skills' – that is, the ability to reflect upon and consider the functions and forms of communication.

In 1962, Jean Piaget was one of the first to shift the focus on play away from social and emotional development and towards cognitive development. Piaget argued that play contributes to intellectual development through the processes of 'accommodation' and 'assimilation'. Assimilation is the dominant mode in play, with children achieving it through play by taking an idea and making it fit with what they know and understand. With the emergence of symbolic play and abstract thinking, evidenced through a child's ability to represent the world, we see the basis for the development of later symbolic behaviours. The symbolic nature of play can be seen as a necessary precursor for other symbolic behaviours such as writing or formal dance.

The theories of Lev Vygotsky (1978) stress the mental representation of symbolic actions and objects as one of the key features of play. He went as far as to say that play is the leading activity of childhood, as it supports all aspects of a child's development. The ability to mentally represent experience, as happens during play, leads to the ability to think in abstract terms, one of the most important facets of human behaviour.

Added to this, Vygotsky stressed the importance of social and cultural factors in the development of play. He noted that make-believe play is socially and culturally determined, and as children explore this type of play they are deepening their understanding of the social life and rules of their communities.

Many others have written about play, and as well as proposing explanations of its function, attempts have been made to categorize play in all its forms. For instance, Mildred Parten, writing in the 1930s, categorized play into the following types: children as onlookers; solitary play as a child plays alone; parallel play, when children play alongside but not with each other; and group play, when children play together.

Corinne Hutt (1979) created a taxonomy of play – attempting to categorize play into different types. According to Hutt, broadly speaking, the three main categories of play are:

- *epistemic play* – within which children learn and explore the world and its properties;
- *ludic play* – when children are using their imaginations but are not learning;
- *games with rules* – structured activities.

The notion of some types of play being of higher value as more is learnt is not an uncommon feature in theories of play. Many theorists describe play when children are engaged in imaginative exploration and creation as lacking in structure and depth. It could be argued that this ascription of lack of value is more about the fact that researchers find, or have found until recently, it very hard to follow, understand and encapsulate children's imaginative free play. Adults, by their very presence, will affect children's play and the introduction of film and video as research tools has provided an additional dimension of investigation into play.

More recently, Tina Bruce (1997) draws on chaos theory as a model for play. When play is at its most fruitful, it is in 'free-flow', she argues.

What this means is that children are solving problems, and symbolically representing their experiences, in ways that are highly creative and spontaneous and of high intellectual order. This requires space, opportunity and safety.

Bruce also offers a critique of the way many other theorists place value on structured play and games with rules, without full appreciation of the value of free-flow play. For Bruce, (1997, 2001) free-flow play:

- is an active process without a product;
- is intrinsically motivated;
- exerts no external pressure to conform to rules, pressures, goals, tasks or definite directions;
- is about possible alternative worlds which involve 'supposing' and 'as if', involving being imaginative, original, innovative and creative;
- is about participants wallowing in ideas, feelings and relationships, involving reflecting on and becoming aware of what we know or 'metacognition';
- actively uses previous first-hand experiences, including struggle, manipulation, exploration, discovery and practice;
- is sustained, and when in full flow, helps us to function in advance of what we can actually do in our real lives;
- requires the use of technical prowess and competencies we have previously developed, allowing us to be in control;
- can be initiated by a child or an adult;
- can be solitary;
- can be in partnership, or groups of adults and/or children, who will be sensitive to each other;
- is an integrating mechanism, which brings together everything we learn, know, feel and understand.

Play and healing

From these perspectives, play can be seen as integral to the process of child development. But what role can it have where development has been interrupted through war, conflict or violence? In this context it is to the psychoanalytic and psychotherapeutic theories of play that we turn.

The theories of the founder of psychoanalytic theory and practice, Sigmund Freud (1856–1939), have been well documented. His view of play was that it allows children to express negative emotions and to reconcile inner anxieties within the unconscious. The notion of 'catharsis' is central to Freud's theories of play. Catharsis is the reconciliation of instinctive urges with the demands and rules of society as internalized by the individual. Play offers an opportunity for children to reach catharsis and so come to terms with traumatic experiences and events by providing a safe way to express difficult feelings. In this way children gain control over their feelings and are able to deal with situations that are stressful or traumatic. Repetitive play is a particularly important part of this process; playing out a situation again and again can lead to resolution of a problem or feeling.

These approaches focus on the internal and emotional worlds of children, and can therefore be seen as particularly relevant when working with children who have been affected by the disruption and disorder of war and civil conflict. Nevertheless, according to Cohen (1993: 150), this focus again works against play being seen holistically, as play is not valued in itself but is seen as a means to an end.

Within the psychoanalytic approach, Susan Isaacs (1926) is an influential figure in child development. Her interest in Freudian analysis stemmed from an early focus on biological psychology. Isaacs trained as an analyst herself. She ran the Malting House School in Cambridge from 1924 until 1927, working with children between the ages of 2 and 8. She meticulously observed the children in her care and captured her observations in her publications. She went on to found the Department of Child Development at the Institute of Education, University of London, and exercised enormous influence on the development of thinking about early childhood in the UK.

Isaacs saw play as means of expressing the total personality but also noted its healing properties as well as its cognitive potential: 'For Isaacs, play was "a bridge", both in the child's emotional development and in his intellectual development' (Cohen 1993: 152).

Anna Freud (1896–1982), the youngest daughter of Sigmund, pioneered the field of child analysis. Having previously run a nursery in Vienna where children were encouraged to play, she moved at the beginning of the Second World War to London, where she founded the Hampstead War Nursery and further developed her theories. Anna Freud's theories were based upon the fact that play reveals the unconscious mind.

Before Anna Freud's arrival in London, Melanie Klein (1882–1960) had been developing work on child analysis, and her interpretation of the therapeutic process differed from Freud's. Freud's arrival led to a split in the British psychoanalytic movement which was resolved when Freud and Klein established separate training courses.

Anna Freud and Melanie Klein both wrote about the therapeutic nature of play and can be seen to be the leading influences in the development of child psychotherapy. Klein developed Freud's work by stating that there is symbolic meaning in *all* aspects of play. The main point in the work of both Freud and Klein is that play reveals tensions but is also the means by which such tensions are resolved.

The work of both Freud and Klein heralded the creation of the child psychotherapy movement and associated play, creative and art therapies. The play therapy movement, as described by Victoria Axline in the classic book, *Dibs: In Search of Self* (1990), which looks in detail at the therapeutic process, can be seen to derive more directly from the work of Klein.

Winnicott (1971), a paediatrician who later became a psycho-analyst, was a colleague of Klein. He interpreted play as the inter-mediary experience between the child's inner world and the outer world. He stressed that play is a normal occupation of childhood which offers a safe space within which inner tensions can be explored in the outer world.

In Winnicott's thinking, play therapy sees play as a healing experi-ence, within which children can solve their problems and resolve inner tensions, hence coming to terms with difficult or overwhelming feelings. Importantly, he noted: 'It is good to remember always that playing is itself a therapy. To arrange for children to be able to play is itself a psychotherapy that has immediate and universal application' (1971: 50).

From the work of Freud, Klein and Winnicott the play therapy movement has developed. The approach stresses the benefits of a dedicated time and space for children to play within the emotional structure created by the play therapist. Many of the concepts and methods of play therapy are now in wide general use in early years and school settings.

A number of stages exist in the therapeutic play process that it may be helpful for early childhood practitioners to note. The stages are:

- *sensory play* – within this type of play, children use a tactile medium such as clay to explore the world through their senses; they can dribble or shape or smear according to their needs;
- *projective play* – is where children use toys and props to tell a story that will indicate their inner concerns and fears;
- *symbolic play* – is where children negotiate roles and stories, clearly indicating when the play is stopping and starting; children can explore difficult feelings, traumas and experiences through this type of play (Cattanach 1994).

The relationship between the therapist and the child is crucial – it has to be based on an empathy that is not intrusive, and a real connection with the child must be present. The child's concerns must be paramount and the therapist must allow space for the child to express themselves.

Cross-cultural theories of play

Finally – and particularly in the context of work with refugee children – it is important to consider whether children's play is a universal phenomenon.

The majority of theorists would argue that it is – all children in all societies appear to engage in activities that would fulfil some of the criteria of play, as described above. That is, children explore and pretend as a way of engaging with the world. More importantly, play everywhere is an 'enculturing' process – that is, a means through which children learn about their cultures: 'Play, a dominant activity of children in all cultures, is viewed to be both a cause and an effect of culture. Play is an expression of a particular culture; play is an important context or vehicle for cultural learning/transmission' (Roopnarine *et al.* 1994: 5).

However, children's play differs in its details in different cultural groups (Roopnarine *et al.* 1994). Researchers into play have attempted to identify those aspects that are universal and those that may be culturally specific. For instance, Haight *et al.* (1999) claim that the universal dimensions of play include the way objects are used, and pretend play. More culturally specific dimensions of play include specific play themes, the extent to which children initiate play with caregivers and the choice of play partners. Haight *et al.* carry on to argue that these differences in play will lead to different developmental pathways for children.

Another important factor when considering cross-cultural dimensions of play is the importance that parents will attribute to the role of play in child development. Hyun (1998) describes how families from European and North American backgrounds tend to emphasize the cognitive importance of play, with an individual perspective on play that is very object- and toy-focused. Meanwhile, families from other backgrounds (although all those researched by Hyun were at that time living in the USA), tend to focus on the social dimensions of play. Therefore, the interactions *within* play, and the *emotional* significance of play, are of greater importance.

In Hyun's study, families not originating from a North American background may also see play and learning as very separate activities.

This is in contrast with prevailing northern European and North American perspectives on play as a tool for learning.

Roopnarine *et al.* (1994) provide a further perspective on the cross-cultural approach, arguing that increasing numbers of researchers are now beginning to question the commonly understood developmental theories of play, especially in terms of children's play as a means to come to explore self in relation to others, with the individual at the centre of development. Instead, Roopnarine and colleagues suggest that in some cultural contexts children are so integrated within a family and community that they may come to understand the family and its web of social relationships before realizing self. What they then argue for in relation to early years services is a sensitivity to and integration of features of the play of children from diverse cultural groups into the early years setting (such as play themes and stories). This they see as an enriching experience for all.

Finally, as Bruce (2001: 15) notes, 'Play looks different in different cultural contexts'. Notable differences include:

- whether or not adults play with children and especially whether they initiate play;
- the point at which children are expected not to play any more – ages will vary across cultures;
- the giving of toys – in some cultures toys are seen as essential props for successful play and so are seen as a central feature of childhood;
- play in mixed age groups away from adults.

Conclusion

We have traced the conditions for optimal development for the child and noted how war and conflict destroy the conditions for child development and erode children's rights, including the right to play.

The importance of the early years has been emphasized via a review of research on early brain development, wherein the earliest relationships help shape children's responses and ability to interact with the world.

So what do these multiple perspectives on play tell us about the role and importance of play in children's lives? We can draw the following conclusions.

First, play is a universal feature of child development and happens in all communities which enjoy safety and security, although attitudes to play and its details will vary.

Second, play is both the way that children express themselves and the means through which they resolve issues. Moreover, play is a means by which children learn and hypothesize about the world. Cultural, social, emotional, cognitive and other areas of developmental progress cannot be disentangled in this process.

We will focus in greater detail on how lessons from play theorists can inform the ways that early childhood practitioners can support young asylum-seeking and refugee children later in the book.

2

BEING A REFUGEE: THE LOSS OF PLAY

I was happy in my country, but then the war started and I saw lots of people die.

> 7-year-old Afghani boy (Save the Children and
> the Refugee Council 2001)

Refugees and asylum-seekers may arrive in the UK or elsewhere traumatized and disorientated, separated from family, forced by persecution to leave their countries and communities. What is the story behind these images of loss and desperation?

Who is a refugee?

According to the United Nations High Commissioner for Refugees (UNHCR) there are just over 20 million refugees and people of concern to UNHCR in the world (United Nations High Commissioner for Refugees (UNHCR) 2004). At least 45 per cent – or more than 9 million – are children under the age of 18.

Techniques of modern warfare mean that civilians are increasingly likely to be the victims of war and civil conflict. It is interesting to note that in the First World War only about 5 per cent of all casualties were civilians. Changes in the capacity and scope of modern weapons now mean that one person can potentially kill many others.

For instance, an automatic rifle such as a Kalashnikov can fire many rounds per minute. This, coupled with the fact that terrorizing whole populations is now seen as a legitimate form of war, means that in today's conflicts almost 90 per cent of casualties are civilians (UNICEF

1996). Genocide, human rights abuses and gender-based violence are all common features of contemporary conflicts.

> Children are not spared. It is estimated that 500,000 under-five-year-olds died as a result of armed conflicts in 1992 alone. In Chechnya, between February and May 1995, children made up an appalling 40 per cent of all civilian casualties; Red Cross workers found that children's bodies bore marks of having been systematically executed with a bullet through the temple. In Sarajevo in Bosnia and Herzegovina, almost one child in four has been wounded.
>
> (UNICEF 1996)

Children can also be particular victims of the technological development of modern weaponry. Landmines now pose a great threat to children in areas of war and civil conflict around the world. According to Amnesty International United Kingdom (1999: 22):

> Millions of the 'anti-personnel' landmines lying unexploded in Cambodia, Afghanistan, Angola, Bosnia, Vietnam, Somalia, Iraq and elsewhere, were spread on or near roads, tracks and footpaths – usually in the countryside. Millions of others were dropped from the air as 'cluster bombs', covering huge areas of land with tiny explosives waiting to be detonated by anyone passing by – soldier or civilian, adult or child. . . . Children are especially susceptible, and the tasks given to children – gathering firewood, tending animal herds or collecting water – make it more likely they will disturb unexploded mines.

Some mines are small, the size of a small ball, and are brightly coloured. They are therefore very attractive to children and bound to arouse their curiosity. The makers of these weapons and the armed forces that employ them are well aware of the nature of their impact and their fatal attraction for children. What commitment is this to the rights of children?

Once war or civil conflict erupt, most refugees will only take flight as far as another part of their own country. Only a small number of those who become refugees reach Europe, and even fewer arrive in the UK.

The term 'refugee' has a specific legal definition. Under the 1951 *United Nations Convention on Refugees* a refugee is someone who has had to leave his or her country 'owing to a well-founded fear of being persecuted for reasons of race, religion, nationality, membership of a particular social group or political opinion'.

An 'asylum-seeker' is a person who has crossed an international border and is seeking safety or protection in another country. In the UK, asylum-seekers are those who have claimed asylum and are waiting a decision by the Home Office, the responsible department of the UK government, as to whether they can remain in the UK or not and be recognised as refugees.

There is a popular view that the UK takes more that its 'fair share' of refugees. Numerical evidence compiled by the voluntary agency working with refugees and asylum-seekers (the Refugee Council 2002) refutes such claims. The Refugee Council argues that 'If you consider global refugee and asylum seeking populations in relation to the host country's size, population and wealth, the UK ranks 32nd. Taking the greatest burden are Iran, Burundi and Guinea'. Even in Europe, the UK was ranked just eighth in terms of numbers of asylum applications calculated in relation to the overall population in 2002.

As must be obvious on reflection, most of the world's refugees will in fact seek safety in the nearest secure place, which is often another part of their own country or a neighbouring country. This means that some of the world's poorest countries are having to cope with the largest number of refugees.

Applications in the UK are received from people from areas of conflict and instability around the world. Most recently, according to the Home Office (2003), the highest number of applications was received from Iraq and then Somalia, Zimbabwe and Afghanistan.

Applications are assessed by the Integrated Casework Unit at the Home Office Immigration and Nationality Directorate. Applicants have to demonstrate that they meet the stipulations of the 1951 *Convention* as described above.

Why do people flee?

Imagine yourself in this situation. You are a mother of four children, 11, 7, 5 and 2 years of age. You live in an area of the world that has experienced increased political instability over the past few years. Civil unrest has recently erupted. Soldiers are now approaching your village and you know that you must gather your children and a few possessions and leave the village in the next hour. You will have to walk into the mountains and so cannot carry very much. What do you feel? What do you tell your children? What few items do you decide to take with you?

Even a few moments contemplating a situation like this enables us to begin to imagine a small fraction of the horror of being forced out of one's home because of circumstances beyond one's control. When considering the fraught circumstances facing many asylum-seekers on arrival in the UK, it is important to be able to step back and take note of why people seek refuge in the first place.

Case study

Mrs X and her three young children left her country after being subject to imprisonment and torture because of Mr and Mrs X's political activities.

Mr X was arrested, tortured and sentenced to 14 years imprisonment for his peaceful activities against the military regime. The security organizations are empowered to arrest without charge and to imprison without trial. After three years of imprisonment, Mr X managed to escape and went into hiding.

Mr X went to prison at a time when Mrs X was pregnant. She too was routinely arrested and tortured both physically and mentally. When she was 8 months pregnant, her torture was to stand on her feet for up to 12 hours a day for a number of days at a time. The result of this was that she developed severe problems in the blood vessels in her legs as well as anaemia. Due to her health problems she had to have a caesarean section without anaesthetic.

Mrs X and her three children tried to seek refuge in Syria where they spent 11 months. Mrs X became ill but the hospital refused to treat her without a passport. The authorities also threatened to take her children away.

Eventually they moved on to the Ukraine where the family were detained again for four days and then sent back to Syria. Some friends of Mrs X's husband managed to get a new (false) passport issued to the family and they returned to the Ukraine. Once again they were unwelcome, so they finally moved to the UK. They had spent one year and three months travelling by the time they arrived. Mrs X's husband is still in hiding.

The effect of the war on the children has been extreme. The eldest son dreams regularly about guns and violence and still sleepwalks, some two years after arrival in the UK. He was referred to a psychiatrist and has also received treatment from a specialist agency working with survivors of torture. The second child also has bad memories and has had a series of behavioural problems at school. The youngest child does not remember a great deal but misses her father. All three children miss their father and have been through periods of blaming their mother for the separation.

The family lived for two years in one room in a large dirty hotel where they experienced a multitude of problems, ranging from mould on the walls (exacerbating asthma in the eldest child), to a broken window (not fixed for six months) to the general overcrowding of sharing a bathroom and kitchen with several other families, with no space for the children to play.

This case study, one of several compiled by the Salusbury World refugee project, based at a school in North London, is not unusual in any way. Torture and harassment are carried out in a routine and psychologically damaging way in many parts of the world. Although the physical experiences can be extreme, survivors of torture also talk about its inevitability, the way it breaks the spirit and the overwhelming feelings of helplessness that come to dominate one's existence. The impact of parental torture on children, while secondary, is still immense. Parents who have been physically and spiritually broken through the experiences of torture may not be able to respond to the need for intimacy and love that children rightly express. Children may become psychologically the strongest members of the family and in so doing forego their childhoods. It is therefore vitally important that children are able to enjoy the safety and security of an environment that will enable them to be children and have opportunities to play.

How many people?

The Refugee Council again notes that people in Britain tend to vastly overestimate the numbers of asylum-seekers and refugees in the UK. According to research conducted by the Refugee Council, on average people think that about a quarter (23 per cent) of the world's refugees and asylum-seekers are in the UK. The reality is that the UK has less than 2 per cent of the world's refugee population.

The Refugee Council goes on to state:

> When comparing the numbers of asylum-seekers granted protection in the UK with those in Canada, the UK emerges as far from being a 'soft touch'. In 2001, Canada granted protection to 97 per cent of Afghan asylum applicants, where the UK granted only 19 per cent. Somali applicants had a 92 per cent success rate in Canada, where in the UK it was only 34 per cent. 85 per cent of Colombian applicants in Canada were granted protection, against a mere 3 per cent in the UK.
>
> (Refugee Council 2002)

In the first few months of 2003, 16,000 applications were received for asylum in the UK. This figure is about a third lower than the equivalent period in 2002. It is worth noting that throughout the whole of 2002, there were 85,865 applications for asylum in the UK. As an individual applies on behalf of dependants this means that applications were received from approximately 110,700 individuals, according to Home Office figures (2003).

What happens once an application is made?

There can be one of three outcomes. The first is that the application is rejected. The second is that temporary agreement is given for an individual to remain in the country. The third is that an individual is granted full refugee status.

When temporary leave is given, after a fixed time the government will then review the political situation in the country of origin and may decide that it is safe to return. The right to temporary admission to the UK was called exceptional leave to remain (ELR), and was often granted for four years, after which an application for indefinite leave to remain could be made (ILR).

More recently, the government has been issuing a temporary protection order of 12 months with no prospect of renewal. And the system has now changed further, with the Home Office no longer granting ELR, but instead granting either 'humanitarian protection' or 'discretionary leave'.

Humanitarian protection is given when the government recognizes that there is a real risk of 'death, torture, or other inhuman or degrading treatment, which falls outside the strict terms of the 1951 Refugee Convention' (Refugee Council 2002). When granted humanitarian protection, three years' temporary leave is given, allowing the applicant access to employment in the same way that someone granted full refugee status is able to work. Entitlement to welfare support is also granted. After three years the application will be reviewed, and if the Home Office feels that protection is no longer needed then arrangements will be made for the applicant to return to their country of origin.

Discretionary leave may be granted when someone making an application is not recognized as being in need of refugee status or humanitarian protection, but it is considered that their removal may cause the worsening of health conditions or may contravene their human rights. It can be granted for any period up to three years. Discretionary leave is granted in some cases for young people under the age of 18. If an applicant is granted discretionary leave this also entitles them to work or to claim welfare benefits and to access other public services.

As can be seen from the description of the various options given here, the rights of children are not fully taken into account in UK asylum legislation. The implications of the current situation are profound. For instance, as humanitarian protection or discretionary leave to remain in the UK is temporary, parents and caregivers will be in a constant state of worry about what will happen next. That worry will be communicated to their children.

Three years is a large proportion of the life of a young child – but because permission to stay is temporary, children may not be included fully in early years settings, for example, or within communities more generally, and therefore may not experience the usual opportunities to play and become part of a community.

The provisions available under UK law are basically about meeting the survival needs of refugees only, and do not address the broader needs – and rights – of all children, to develop their learning and play. On the other hand, if the refugee child has been able to experience relationships and play opportunities, and the re-establishment of trust and security which those will assist in fostering, then the removal of these opportunities from a child is potentially very harmful.

Discretionary leave to remain in the UK may place even more pressures upon a family, as it may well be granted for shorter periods of time.

In 2002, 12 per cent of all initial applications resulted in the granting of full refugee status. In addition, 29 per cent of applicants were given exceptional leave to remain (ELR), meaning that 41 per cent of all applications were successful. In addition, 21 per cent of all appeals were successful. These figures run counter to the public perception, fostered by the media, that all applications are unjustified or 'bogus', and that great numbers of people are making false claims. In fact it is clear that many of those applying for asylum are being successfully recognized as refugees with well-founded claims. And again, bearing in mind the extreme situations that many families and children will have experienced, the burden of having to prove that they have a well-founded fear of persecution in order to justify their asylum claims will create a lot of stress and tension in a family.

Where applications are refused, this can be for many reasons. One of the most common is the incorrect completion of paperwork. As applying for refugee status is complex it is not surprising that people who often will not be able to understand or read English, even when working with a translator and solicitor, are not always able to fill in all forms correctly.

The current situation

There is current controversy over the implementation of Home Office plans to consider applications for asylum only from those people who make their application at the place or port of entry into the UK.

In the past, people would often arrive in the UK and make an application either on arrival or after having been in the country for a few days, when they might have been enquiring about the details of what they needed to do and where they needed to go in order to make their claim. Now, the government has decided it will provide no resources at all for the support of those who apply for asylum after they have entered the country.

This move has led a large number of agencies to voice concern about the plight of those denied all forms of support. The Refugee Council has reported the impact of this ruling as resulting in hundreds of people being forced to sleep rough, in parks or on the streets, hungry and homeless. Indeed there have been reports of men and women forced to sleep outside the offices of the Refugee Council in South London, waiting for Church and other groups to bring food in vans, unable to access toilet facilities, with no means of keeping warm or clean. At the time of writing this latest asylum ruling by the government is still being disputed in the courts.

It is important to note that a family with children under the age of 18 should always be offered support by the government's National Asylum Support Service (NASS).

Those who make an application on arrival become the responsibility of the NASS, which will provide accommodation and support for those awaiting the outcome of their application. As readers may be aware from television or other news reports, asylum applicants are dispersed around the country. The initial reason for this was to remove pressure on local authorities in London and the South East.

In the past, when new arrivals came to the UK they would normally try to find relatives or friends and stay with them while their claims were processed. This meant that refugee communities would emerge in particular areas in many of the large cities in the UK. For instance, there is a thriving Somali community in South Wales and a Kurdish community in North London. New arrivals would find community organizations and informal support systems in place, and applicants would find a temporary place of safety within the community. Children would be able to join with other children from the wider community and perhaps gain access to play and early years provision.

However, some local authorities felt that they were being disproportionately penalised by having to provide housing and other welfare services in such areas. Therefore, in 1998 the government introduced the Asylum and Immigration Act. A new policy of dispersal was introduced which has resulted in new arrivals being dispersed to accommodation around the country. This accommodation is privately-owned or run by voluntary organizations or housing associations.

When this step was first introduced it provoked further distress among asylum-seekers who had already experienced hardship. For instance, families would be dispersed to areas without a history of good community relations, to live in housing that was not always of a high standard. Families would be very isolated in communities where there might be only a very few people from their country of origin. It proved hard for them to find familiar food or food that was required for religious reasons such as halal meat, and places of worship were not always close by. In addition, local host communities were sometimes hostile.

Many local authorities and community groups have worked hard to put into place good support systems. However, some families still face isolation and harassment, with reports of children being attacked, and graffiti and other forms of abuse routinely directed at asylum-seekers. The conditions in some temporary accommodation can also be difficult for families, as the following examples reveal.

For instance, one family were living in a hostel for almost two years, waiting for the results of their application. The parents and three girls were sharing one room that contained a very small gas hob, a sink and a shower. Beds had to be put up each night and taken down during the day. There was no space for the children to play.

The parents were often concerned about letting the girls use the toilet as it was outside the room and shared by all the other occupants of the corridor, was rarely cleaned and often did not work. A number of other people in the hostel had alcohol or drug problems and the parents were very concerned about the welfare of their children. Another child graphically described her temporary hotel home:

> I don't like living in the hotel because it smells. When we come in and it's raining outside there is nowhere to put our wet clothes. There is nowhere for me to do my homework, so I do it on the bed. It's noisy because my little brothers and sisters are playing.
>
> It's small and difficult to sleep because we all sleep in the same room. There are people shouting at night. We can't have people to visit so my friends can't come and play. The toilet is in the bathroom and it smells. Lots of people use the kitchen and it's too small and it's difficult to do the cooking for our family.
>
> We have to keep the rubbish bin in our bedroom. It smells and my brother keeps bumping into it. We can't hear the TV because it is too noisy outside.
>
> (Salusbury World and Save the Children 2004: 121)

In addition, a number of centres exist around the country where some applicants are detained while their applications are processed, making it easy for them to be removed if their applications fail. Those detained have often come from countries the Home Office deems not to be dangerous – so that any applications for asylum from individuals from such countries are immediately thought not to be warranted.

Children and families are also held in these centres, and in Dungavel, Lanarkshire in Scotland, campaigners have been arguing for children held at the centre to be allowed to have access to education in local schools. According to a report in the *Guardian* newspapers (15 August 2003), 'The Ay family, with four children aged eight to 14, were held at Dungavel for more than a year before being deported to Germany last week. Beriwan Ay, 14, had spoken of the children's distress at being kept in Dungavel, unable to play freely and denied access to a proper education'. Dungavel, the report went on, was the only immigration detention centre in Britain regularly to hold children for long periods: 'The welfare and development of children is likely to be compromised by detention, however humane the provisions, and that will increase the longer detention is maintained'. Anne Owers, the Chief Inspector of Prisons, believed that independent assessors should be brought in to decide if conditions were suitable for children to be detained.

There were 18 youngsters at the privately run centre at the time of Owers' inspection. Families were locked into the 62-bed family unit and had to ask to be let out to visit the centre's shop, while there was limited access to outdoor play areas for children.

Cole (2003), in research into the detention of asylum-seeking families in the UK, records the impact of detention on families in greater detail. According to Cole's study, arrest or removal from home impacted seriously on young children. In one example, a mother described how eight police officers came to the house at half past six in the morning. While being transported from Manchester to Gatwick, her 2-year-old son needed to use the toilet. The police refused to stop.

Security staff were also described as behaving forcefully: 'They put handcuffs on my hands . . . my children crying on the floor [beside me]', one mother reported (Cole 2003: 46).

Cole also describes how 'people explained how settled they had become in this country. Two families explained that their children's first language was now English, with one father extremely concerned that his children were facing removal to a country they had never known' (p. 25). Some families had been in the UK for up to six years, and were being uprooted from communities and friendships.

Cole also goes on to note that detention is experienced as a particular blow to families who have had a difficult journey to the UK – only then to have their claims rejected. As one mother says: '[My children were] just four and a half years and one year old when we left. All together in a lorry. Take medication for sleeping because is maybe cry, my children. Yes it was very difficult . . . I stay in detention centre my whole life [rather than go back]' (p. 31).

The impact on children is also noted, as one mother says of her 18-month-old daughter and another child: '[My daughter] . . . It's not good to put kids in detention. Sometimes she'll be playing, and she just starts crying. She scared about the police . . . A little eight year old, he said [to staff in Harmondsworth] "Going to take the gun, and kill you, and leave here with my mum". He said "I miss my dad" ' (p. 36).

Cole also notes the lack of play and educational facilities in some of the centres. For instance, in one centre, not specifically designed for families, children were only allowed to play outside for between 20 minutes and an hour a day. And an older girl notes how her 5-year-old brother was not able to bring any toys to the centre, and how he really missed them.

Save the Children and other children's organizations have been campaigning to ensure that the rights of asylum-seeking children are effectively recognized. Drawing on the terms of the *UNCRC* – United Nations Convention on the Rights of the Child – they are putting the argument that as children first and foremost, asylum-seeking children should not be made to suffer the consequences of changes in asylum legislation. Children's rights under the *UNCRC*, to play and to education, are being denied despite the fact that the UK government is a signatory to the *Convention* and therefore has a duty under international law to act to ensure that the rights of all children are upheld.

Children as asylum-seekers and refugees

Children may well have lost parents and been subject to, or witnesses of, violence. Children may also have been displaced, spent time in hiding and have been subject to shelling and attack.

Journeys to safety can also have been perilous. Families may have had to walk long distances with their belongings without much food or water before finding a place of safety. Refugee camps, although providing some safety and security, can also be dangerous places. The risk of sexual violence can be high, and women and girls can fall victim to armed gangs who control access to resources.

Journeys to countries such as the UK are often dangerous and are undertaken through illegal means. This is because it is virtually impossible to gain visas or papers to travel legally when a country is at war or experiencing civil conflict. Therefore, using forged passports and payments of large amounts of money to traffickers are often the only route to safety for some people.

This can be extremely dangerous for all involved. While these experiences can be terrifying for adults they also take their toll on children. Some children may have been required to stay quiet and still for long periods – others may even have been given medication to quieten them.

Teachers and other carers in early years settings may come across children playing out similar experiences to those described above. The temptation may by to stop children from doing this. However, it is by playing out these scenarios that children transform their experiences into manageable situations. As individuals they regain a sense of control and agency and can again be assertive and proactive in their lives.

Issues facing asylum-seeking and refugee communities

Refugee communities are diverse. Within one national group, asylum-seekers and refugees may come from a wide range of class, religious, political, educational and ethnic backgrounds.

Some families will have suffered traumatic experiences in their home countries. For a small number of children and adults, this may affect their ability to cope and rebuild their lives. Parents may be emotionally absent and unable therefore to give their children the attention they need – for instance by supporting and encouraging play.

At the same time there may be negative social reactions to the presence of refugees in their new homes. The terms 'beggars', 'scroungers' and 'bogus' are all too familiar in some parts of the UK media, when referring to asylum-seekers in particular. This negative press coverage has an impact on children and families, with evidence of even very young children being abusive to refugee and asylum-seeking peers.

In addition, refugee families are likely to have suffered a drop in their standard of living, as well as other major changes in their lives which can contribute to psychological vulnerability. The experience of exile can also mean that many refugee women have lost their support networks of extended family and friends. This is particularly an issue for mothers of young children who may feel extremely isolated. In some refugee groups it is not uncommon to find that a disproportionate number of households are headed by women. There are many lone mothers in the Somali community, for instance, because so many men have been killed in the fighting. This again has an impact on children, as the emotional impact of living in exile and in isolation, with a lone parent, may well be very difficult to deal with. And for the parent, given the weight of dealing with the needs of the family single-handedly, it may again be hard to respond appropriately to children's emotional needs and requirements for play.

A recent report produced by the agency Refugee Action, *Is it Safe Here?* (2003), highlights the experiences of women refugees in the UK. According to the report women represent about a third of all applications for asylum to the UK, however women find themselves quickly isolated and often facing abuse, and have an enormous struggle integrating.

One refugee group estimates that half of the women they have had contact with have been raped or sexually assaulted before reaching the UK. In addition, many of these women, some of whom were now experiencing medical and psychological distress, were not aware of the services in this country that could support them.

However, once in the UK, women also face a catalogue of prejudice and harassment. Many women said they were too afraid to go out and had experienced verbal or physical abuse on the streets. One woman said a neighbour had flicked lit cigarettes at her children, while local youths regularly threw stones at her windows.

Another issue is that some women will have had to leave their children in the care of relatives in order to flee to a place of safety. This clearly causes particular stress to a woman and is estimated to be the experience of about 40 per cent of single women refugees in the UK.

Other women face a different experience, where they are caring for children without the support of their partners. In addition, fewer than one in five of those interviewed described their English as good. While almost all the women said they wanted to improve their English, half said they could not attend classes because of a lack of childcare.

It is important to be aware of the educational and care services that asylum-seeking and refugee children have a *right* to use. They are entitled to access educational services during the ages of statutory schooling (5–16), and can also use pre-school services. Children whose parents are supported under the NASS arrangements are also entitled to free school meals.

Access to early years provision and play ∎

Despite this entitlement, it remains the case for early years provision that asylum-seeking and refugee children are often under-represented in such services. This is also true in a range of other play and leisure activities such as after school and sports activities.

This can be for a variety of reasons. Parents and carers are often unfamiliar with the services that are available for young children; this sort of provision would not have been available in their countries of origin, where extended family members would normally care for the youngest children and formal schooling starts at age 6 or 7. In addition, in the UK, many different types of early years service exist; for instance, playgroups, parent and child drop-ins, crèches, nursery schools and children's centres to name but a few. This in itself can be confusing for parents, particularly where many services are publicized through word of mouth, or via leaflets in English. It is hard for parents who do not speak English to find out about services as they are not part of local networks.

Waiting lists can be many months long and newly-arrived parents have no opportunity to access such lists. For these reasons and a range of others, including even the small charges that some groups make, very young children from asylum-seeking and refugee families will not always be present in early years groups, despite living in the area, and being in particular need of the service and the play opportunities on offer.

Research has demonstrated the interest in childcare and early childhood services that exists in refugee communities (Rutter and Hyder 1998). This is because refugee families are strongly motivated to ensure that their children receive the best possible provision and make the best possible start. However, it is important to be aware of the diversity of views in relation to play. In many communities and cultures play is taken for granted as something children engage in without adult interference. Children are often in multi-age groups of siblings and extended family, where older children act as play guides to the younger ones. The case for play does not have to be made; it goes on regardless.

Within predominantly urban communities such as those in the UK, where families are more isolated and children are not always exposed to wider age groups, opportunities for play have become more formalized. It is very important that the value of play is conveyed to parents, and especially to asylum-seeker and refugee parents whose children may benefit in particular from the healing experience of play.

Research conducted by the Refugee Council and Save the Children with refugee families, focusing on early years practice and policy (Rutter and Hyder 1998) highlighted the following issues.

Asylum-seeking and refugee families often have multiple issues to contend with. These can include poverty, family separation, difficult legal applications, isolation and psychological trauma. In addition, family members may have particular health requirements due to conflict in the country of origin or medical conditions exacerbated by journeys to safety.

Unfortunately, racism is also a particularly common occurrence. As one Kurdish mother noted: 'Around here the people were against us when we first came. They broke our windows and the police came'.

At the time the research was conducted, the need for childcare and early years provision was not being met, as a survey of a number of local authorities with sizeable refugee populations revealed.

Refugee families will, on average, have a greater number of young children under the age of 5 than the population as a whole. Many adults in the refugee community are in, or would like to access, education and training. Therefore early years services are vitally important. At the same time, early years services offer an opportunity to create a dialogue with parents to discuss their views on play, development and learning.

As a first step to breaking down the isolation many women experience, the provision of childcare to enable them to attend English language classes is essential. However, the research revealed that different local authority departments did not always work together to identify refugee communities, and childcare places were not always available.

However, government initiatives such as Sure Start, and the local authority-based Early Years Development and Childcare Partnerships, have been required to identify particular minority communities such as refugees and asylum-seekers in their planning exercises. Research is still required to ascertain whether such initiatives are effectively reaching refugee and asylum-seeking communities.

Earlier research from the Daycare Trust in 1995 revealed a similar picture. Research into daycare needs was carried out by and about members of the refugee communities from the Horn of Africa (Somalia, Ethiopia and Eritrea), and results comparable to those in the later study were produced.

However, this research also drew attention to the fact that many refugee mothers felt uncomfortable leaving very young children in the care of those who were not part of their own community. Carers were concerned that differences in childrearing practices – for instance, whether a child is left to cry or not, feeding and toileting – would be too great. There was also some concern expressed about the focus on play, apparently at the expense of more formal approaches to learning.

What this points to is the need for the recruitment and training of women from a range of refugee communities to provide childcare to meet the demands from others in the community, and to be a bridge between newer members of the community and early years services.

This issue also linked to concerns that many parents expressed about the need for children to retain a sense of identity. Unlike other migrants, many refugees hope to return one day to their country of origin. It can be extremely distressing for parents when children who are brought up in a country of refuge start to acquire the values and customs of their new home.

From a child's perspective this is perhaps inevitable, and many children successfully manage complex identities and acquire what they feel is positive from each community. For many parents though the gap between family and cultural practices in the country of origin and youth culture in the UK is too great, and becomes yet another loss in the catalogue of losses that can make up the experience of exile.

Another gap in expectations relates to the experience and values of school in the UK. In many communities teachers generate huge respect within a community, parents have little contact with school and education itself is a formal and serious exercise. The contrast with the apparently informal nature of schools within the UK is difficult for some parents to come to terms with. Expectations about behaviour, homework, child-centred curricula and the home–school relationship can cause tensions.

Parents also pointed out that other differences between their customary childcare practices and those common in the UK made them feel uncomfortable. For instance, it is common practice in many parts of the world for younger children to be left in the care of an older sibling. However, in the UK this is not common practice, and parents were concerned that they might be accused of abuse or neglect.

Different expectations of children and views of childhood were also noted by some refugee parents as potential causes of tension. As one mother said: 'At home, an eight-year-old could cook a meal. Now they can't do anything. They just watch television all day'.

Conclusion

In conclusion, this chapter has set out the international and national legal frameworks relating to claiming refugee status. It has also looked at some of the experiences facing children and families caught in the process of claiming refuge in the UK.

The limitations on children's rights to play and education caused by the asylum process have also been explored. The potential clash of values and expectations of asylum-seeking and refugee parents with early years and developmental theory as practiced in the UK has also been considered.

The chapter has set out the case for play in even stronger terms, as a means through which children can overcome some of the losses they may have experienced during the upheaval of seeking asylum. Overall, this chapter has considered the extensive changes that families may have experienced in their journeys to safety and illustrated that those changes do not stop once a place of safety has been reached.

3

THE IMPACT OF WAR, CONFLICT AND VIOLENCE ON YOUNG CHILDREN: THE CONSEQUENCES FOR PLAY

The term 'war' derives from the German noun 'werra' meaning 'confusion' or 'strife'. It is an apt root that provides the world with a picture of what war can do to individuals.

(Elbedour *et al*. 1993: 805)

. . . up until the mid 20th century, little attention was paid to women or children in the literature of war at all.

(Elbedour *et al*. 1993: 806)

This chapter will consider a range of research findings, mainly drawing on evidence from conflict zones worldwide, about the ways conflict and war impact on the development and play of young children.

Refugee children's experiences will vary: some will have directly witnessed violence towards themselves or members of their family, while others will have fled a potentially volatile or violent political environment. Children may have seen the death or torture of family members, and may even have been subject to attack themselves.

Many may have lived under siege, in hiding, perhaps living in basements as their homes and villages were shelled and attacked. They may have experienced the loss of members of their families and perhaps have witnessed or even participated in violent acts themselves.

Family life and school or early years and play routines will have been disrupted. The threat or real experience of violence will have had a severe impact on the child. Asylum-seeking and refugee children may well have experienced loss, trauma and change to an extreme degree.

What happens to children?

We will now turn to the evidence from research about the impact of war and violence on the child.

From the outset, it is important to bear in mind that much of the literature comes from North American or European based researchers. What this may mean is that assumptions are made about children and those factors and conditions that constitute a normal childhood. Many communities and cultures have very different ways of understanding health, well-being and childhood (Boyden and Mann 2000) and will have specific ways of dealing with adversity and stress that might focus on the group or community rather than the individual child.

There are also cultural perspectives evident in the way that events and responses are interpreted (UNICEF 1993). For instance, dreams in many cultures and communities are profound and important events, while for others in different parts of the world dreams are minimal, incidental events (Bracken 1998). The point is that it is the meaning that we ascribe to events that gives them power and force, and meaning differs from community to community. Therefore, when considering the literature on the impact of conflict and violence on children it is important to think about whether all the findings are applicable to all children in all situations. This is not to minimize the terrible experiences that children have in situations of war and conflict, but it is to say that there are different responses and meanings ascribed to the events themselves and also to any interventions:

> Every culture has its own unique explanations for, understandings of and expectations of life experiences, including traumatic experiences. What causes stress in one tradition may not cause the same stress in another. Cultural explanations influence how causes of distress are understood, the ways in which events and personal reactions to such events are described, the symptoms and behaviours adopted to respond to stress, as well as preferred treatments.
>
> (UNICEF 1993: 173)

It can be argued that the restoration of opportunities to play in an early years setting, while remaining potentially healing for the individual child, is a community-based response to violence and conflict that removes attention away from the individual needs of the child and towards a reconnection with community that is healing for the whole family.

The secondary impact of war, conflict and violence on the infant and young child

The evidence about the impact of war, conflict and violence on young children is varied and there appears to be no clear consensus. It is important to note that individual experiences and interpretations of events will be context-specific but that some responses may be common.

Work by Cassie Landers (1998) for the children's rights organisation UNICEF, provides a useful overview of this topic. Landers identified three main areas of impact when considering the effect of violence on children. These are:

- behavioural manifestations;
- clinical manifestations;
- spiritual and psychological impact.

According to Landers, behavioural manifestations derive from the sensory overload resulting from the chaos of conflict coupled with the fast pace of developmental progression. As she notes, 'a young child's mechanisms for coping with exposure to violence may interfere with the child's primary developmental task – learning' (1998: 9). She goes on to draw on evidence to identify the different ways that children of varying ages may respond to violence.

Clinical and spiritual manifestations vary according to age. Children from birth to 3 may respond to the cues given by the adults around them in an environment dominated by violence by becoming extremely watchful and over-attentive. Children's need to know what is going on around them may detract from their focus on exploration of their immediate environments and from taking pleasure from playing and the normal routines of life.

They may also cling to their carers, wanting to maintain bodily contact, and be generally restless and unsettled, possibly having sleep problems. As infants grow and become more aware of the dangers and tensions in their environments they may start to demonstrate specific reactions. These may include random destructive or aggressive behaviours and the voicing of generalized fears about the world.

Children may also regress and revert to earlier behaviours. Again as children's energy is focused on dealing with the immediate threats surrounding them, their immediate developmental progress will be interrupted and they will not have the energy to explore and learn about the world.

From the age of 3 onwards children may experience extreme fears about their environments. Their powers of imagination, strength of feeling and theories about the world are such that they may even believe that they are *responsible* for events around them. Again the normal playful engagement of young children with their everyday worlds may be interrupted and young children will not be following usual developmental routes.

Table 3.1 shows Landers' categorization of young children's reactions to traumatic events.

Table 3.1   Children's reactions to traumatic events

Infants	Toddlers	Preschool
Withdrawal	Fears	Fears
Clinging	Aggression	Traumatic fantasies
Restlessness	Destructive behaviour	Grief and mourning
	Regression	Guilt feelings
		Creating stories
		Social withdrawal

Source: Landers (1998: 10).

The impact of war, conflict and violence on carers ■

Young children rely on the adults around them to care for them. Children's early lives are dependent on carers' sensitivities and abilities to anticipate their needs. The experience of living in conflict or of being politically oppressed causes enormous stresses for everyone.

This means that carers may, through no fault of their own, be preoccupied and stressed, and even depressed, and may not be in a position to really focus on children's many emotional and social needs. Add to this the experience of leaving one's country of origin and seeking asylum in an unsympathetic country, and it is not surprising that the carers of young asylum-seeking and refugee children are not always able to offer the emotional support or attention that children need in order to thrive.

The key to dealing with stress and conflict for younger children appears to be response of adults – and in particular the mother or primary carer – to the stress of upheaval. The mother becomes 'a protective shield' (Khan 1963: 291 in Elbedour *et al.* 1993: 810).

Numerous studies on children's responses to stress, focusing on conflict in Vietnam, Cambodia and Northern Ireland, reveal that it is primarily the response of families that will enable a child to manage these difficult situations. As noted by Silber (1958: 160 in Elbedour *et al.* 1993: 811), 'the child looks towards the parent for a ready-built perception or structure of the event – a cue from which to determine his own actions and feelings'.

The emotional impact of violence, conflict and oppression will vary from child to child, community to community. As already noted, in some cases children may have witnessed or been directly subject to violence. In many other cases, the impact of violence on children is a secondary one, in the sense that they will absorb the emotional states of the adults and carers around them.

Interrupted developmental processes

It is important to understand the developmental processes that have been interrupted when young children have experienced change, loss and disruption – experiences common to refugee families.

Trust

Small infants learn to trust their mothers and fathers and other primary caregivers to provide food, affection and protection. The direct or indirect impact of violence on children's lives erodes trust and reduces opportunities to explore the environment. Children's basic physical and emotional needs will not necessarily have been met. Life may have been chaotic and unpredictable, leading the child to experience the world as unsafe.

Competence

Children gain confidence through the exploration of their environment via play. But violence or the threat of violence promotes fear and insecurity, and disrupts education and other community activities. If children have been unable to play or to form lasting relationships and friendships in the family or in wider groups in the community, many skills and abilities will have been lost or delayed. Opportunities for the development of physical skills such as running and jumping can be lost if children are confined for their safety or are restricted.

Identity

The sense of self develops throughout childhood, the result of a confident belief in oneself and an understanding of one's place in the community. The refugee experience can undermine self-confidence and self-esteem. Adults' feelings of uncertainly about the family's place in the world will be communicated to the children.

The concept of trauma

There is an extensive literature on the impact of trauma on adults. Debates have been conducted for some time about the validity of concepts such as post-traumatic stress disorder (PTSD) in response to events such as disaster, war and torture. These debates are important to consider, as much of the thinking about appropriate interventions for children is influenced by the conceptualization of the impact of violence on adults.

PTSD describes a range of responses to extreme events. While likely to be severe in adults, its impact is potentially even more damaging to a child's emerging social and emotional development, as extreme events can affect the developmental process.

It is important to remember that a trauma is out of the ordinary; it is an exceptional action or set of events that generate huge amounts of emotion. It violates norms and affects expectations about the future (Gordon and Wraith 1993).

The argument relating to whether PTSD is a valid concept or not is well captured as follows:

> PTSD is often presented as though it was something 'discovered' by psychiatrists, something, which since being discovered, throws lights on other unexplained areas of psychological functioning. In fact, PTSD is something created by psychiatry at a particular historical and cultural moment. This is not to say that the suffering, which the PTSD concept attempts to capture, is in any way fictional or unreal. It is not to say that in the past people did not suffer in the wake of life threatening or deeply distressing events. It is to assert that PTSD is one particular way of approaching and understanding the sequelae of such events.
>
> (Bracken 1998: 39)

The notion of trauma itself is rejected by some researchers; the argument here is that the concept is too individualistic and pathologizes the individual who after all is not manifesting signs of mental illness but is 'showing a normal response to a set of extreme circumstances and requires support rather than psychological treatment' (Richman 1996: 18). What this means is that, while reviewing the available literature on the impact of war and conflict on children which holds trauma as a central notion, it is worth noting that this interpretation of responses to the events of war and conflict is located in one particular cultural context, and may be interpreted differently in different contexts. This also means that solutions such as individual therapy will not necessarily be appropriate; instead, interventions that have meaning for the wider community may be more relevant. Having said this, we will now go on to review the literature on trauma and children.

Trauma, children and play

Again, Landers (1998: 12) covers the ground well:

> Trauma can alter the quality of the young child's play in several ways. Some traumatised children are quite restricted in their range of play activities. Many traumatised children are initially unable to use play symbolically. Trauma may have interrupted developmental processes to the extent that symbolic capacities were not generated. Early relationships may have been disrupted, preventing the child from using transitional objects and other toys as symbols for significant people and experiences. Some traumatised children have developed symbolic capacity to a certain extent, by the quality of their symbolic play is quite unlike that of most young children. Gone is the sense of joyful adventure, story and spirited imaginative discovery that is characteristic of childhood. The play of the remotest child is often grim and despairing. It tends to lack organisation and elaboration. Disturbing themes might be introduced but never resolved in the context of play. Traumatised children's play can become repetitive – the child is driven to play and replay his traumatic experiences in a compulsive attempt to master them. In addition, defences against re-experiencing feelings associated with the trauma may be evident in play.

There are a range of symptoms associated with trauma in children (Pynoos and Nader 1993; Landers 1998). These include:

- *Re-experiencing the event* – this can take the form of flashbacks, dreams and overwhelming memories. In young children these are likely to be manifest as repetitive dreams or play. Landers (1998: 35) proposes that 'children's dreams reflect both their cognitive processing of information and an effort to contend with life's issues. Thus their dreams may provide an indication of what is left over from conscious, over-processing during awake time. Dreams, like play, indicate the child's attempts to gain control over events. For some children, their play, art, storytelling, and social interaction are laced with themes of the events'.

- *Reduced reactions* – in order to cope with overwhelming events, desensitization to the environment is another typical response. Lack of reaction and lack of interest in everyday events is one aspect of this; the other is poor memory and inattentiveness to detail. The message is that nothing really matters.
- *Being on guard* – this refers to the need for children to be constantly aware of their environments and to be constantly on the alert for danger. This results in anxiety, phobia or aggression and depression dependent on the character of the child. Again the psychological strain of this state means that children's normal development is interrupted as their energies and attentions are directed towards survival.

Play is clearly a crucial process through which a child develops. When normal development is interrupted and a child is no longer able to play, all aspects of a child's development are then affected, including cognitive, physical and psychosocial aspects.

The impact of not being able to play means that a child is not able to explore, assimilate and actively build a picture of their immediate world that encompasses all their senses and thinking. Trauma interrupts and skews a child's development by preventing play – and can affect play itself.

Having considered some of the general impacts of conflict and violence on young children, we will now turn to some specific evidence from case studies and research projects.

Children do not forget

According to recent research, and contrary to the views held by many adults, children do *not* forget about bad experiences more easily than adults, and they do *not* 'grow out' of remembering extreme experiences. What they may do is cease speaking about events and issues in response to cues from the adults around them. Indeed, some researchers, such as Gordon and Wraith (1993), believe that children collude with adults to the point that adults are convinced that children no longer remember:

> For many of the adults I spoke to it was hard that children – especially very young children – had lived through the same, brutal events. From the perspective of some parents it was easier to hope that young children had forgotten everything. But we met children who reminded their parents about past events. As one seven year old girl from Srebenica said to her mother, who was describing the hardship of life on arrival at a resettlement camp: 'No . . . that was not the worst. The worst was when we were in the concentration camp and when we fled through the forest'.
>
> In Bosnia when interviewing families about emergency early childhood centres that had been set up during and just after civil conflict I met with a group of families in an area of the country that had seen particularly fierce armed conflict. Children told us how their memories did not go away. One six year old boy referred to 'The pictures in my forehead' and another said 'It is like having a camera in my head'. This watchfulness was also noticed by adults – as one mother said, 'The children always watch us. They are like video cameras taking in everything without explanation'.
>
> (Hyder, Save the Children, unpublished report 1998)

It is clear that children who have seen or experienced violence or other frightening events react in various ways. Some become timid or withdrawn; others become watchful, always alert to the next danger; others copy the violent behaviour they have seen and are themselves aggressive.

The literature on children affected by conflict

Research has been carried out, over the years, with a number of groups of children who have been directly or indirectly exposed to armed conflict (Burlingham and Freud 1942; Pynoos and Nader 1993). These studies include research into the children of torture victims; those who are the children of concentration camp prisoners; children who have themselves lived in camps; and those who have experienced armed conflict.

The children studied here tend to be aged 5 and over, and it is from these studies that we must extract information that will provide an insight into the experiences of younger children. However, these studies do give a clear indication of the emotional consequences of armed conflict and civil unrest on children.

This type of research is often carried out following the family's arrival in a place of safety, which may be a new country where the family is seeking refuge. Issues of identity and adjustment to a new culture and community are also being dealt with as children come to terms with their past experiences and new lives.

Nevertheless, there appear to be a number of shared symptoms experienced by children who have had direct or indirect experience of armed conflict. These symptoms range from fear of loud and unexpected noises, to insomnia and extreme reactions to people in uniform.

Children may experience disturbed sleep and dream of death, murder and abduction. Some children wet their beds, or become depressive and introverted. Others lose their appetite and have stomach-aches or headaches. Difficulties concentrating, poor memory and aggression are also common problems (Krogh and Montgomery 1993).

Krogh and Montgomery (1993) also studied the impact of being the child of torture survivors. Children aged between 5 and 13, from families from around the world, all of whose parents had experienced torture, revealed a range of physical and emotional symptoms including headaches, anxiety, eating problems, depression and difficulties with family relationships. The research study also revealed the coping mechanisms that children adopted to deal with the situation they found themselves in. The strategies included:

- attention-seeking behaviour;
- refusal to acknowledge problems and a need to be alone;
- a need to cut off and daydream;
- a need to seek approval and be good.

The strategy adopted appeared to be dependent on family and cultural norms, age, gender and the child's personality.

Another reported response is that of children identifying with the aggressor. This can take many forms. In essence, children witness the powerlessness of their parents in response to, for instance, soldiers coming to the house. This can be a terrifying experience for children who need to see their parents as powerful in order to feel safe. Identifying with the aggressor is a way of trying to feel powerful and safe. In young children this can also take the form of blaming the parents for not protecting them. For example, a mother of a 4-year-old girl described her daughter's anger when, as a result of growing ethnic tensions, neighbours burnt down their house: 'Why didn't you smile at them Mummy and then they wouldn't have tried to hurt us?' was the daughter's question to her mother a few days after the event.

Children may also blame themselves for what has happened, especially if their parents are depressed or angry: 'Young children may feel that they have caused their parents' withdrawal as a result of their own angry thoughts and actions . . . Young children thinking magically, believe that they have much greater influence over what happens to them than is actually the case' (Melzak 1992: 206).

When they have witnessed violence, very young children may have confused memories about what has happened, in that they are less likely to be able to express in words what they have felt than older children or adults. However, this does not mean that they will have forgotten and they will certainly be affected by what has happened. They need opportunities to sort out their thoughts – for example, through play and other means of self-expression which we will consider in later chapters.

The evidence of the impact of violence caused by conflict and war on children is sparse – but the results are consistent. What is clear is that a small minority of children are severely affected by such experiences. For the majority though, recovery is possible. This is demonstrated through work from a number of conflict zones over recent years.

For instance, UNICEF (1993: 168) cite a number of studies including the work of Bodman in 1941 who surveyed 8000 children in war-torn Britain and noted that about 4 per cent of the children surveyed demonstrated signs of 'strain' following air raids. In a study conducted in 1981, McWhirter (in UNICEF 1993) surveyed the teachers of over 5000 children in Northern Ireland. Just under 9 per cent were reported by teachers to be disturbed, with the disturbance characterized by antisocial behaviour. A report from the Lebanon by Hourani *et al.* (1982) (reported in UNICEF 1993) revealed that about 8 per cent of those taking part in a household study reported 'psychological stress symptoms during conflict'.

How war hurts children

The fallout of armed conflict affects children in many different ways (Amnesty International 1999: 32):

- *Nutritional deprivation* – conflicts often cause famines, with food production and distribution systems destroyed or disrupted.
- *Spread of disease* – communicable diseases are the major cause of death among children in peacetime. In wars, the risks multiply as

water and food supplies are damaged and health services disrupted.

- *Psychological damage* – especially if children have directly witnessed or been involved in acts of violence.
- *Disability* – around 4 million child survivors of conflicts in the past decade have been permanently disabled and landmines continue to kill and maim.
- *Loss of education* – schools are frequently closed in wars, and are even destroyed as a key part of the social fabric. Displacement adds to further disruption.
- *Child combatants* – children who have lost their parents or who come from disrupted families are more likely to become soldiers.
- *Violence against girls* – rape is featured in almost every armed conflict and is common in camps of the displaced. In some conflicts, rape is used as a systematic weapon of terror.
- *Child abduction, torture and slavery* – children kidnapped by armies are frequently beaten and either forcibly enlisted as combatants or enslaved.
- *Child war criminals* – children are often involved in acts of violence. Sometimes this may be a deliberate tactic to ensure communal complicity in atrocities.

The loss of the right to a normal childhood, including the right to play, must also be noted as one of the primary casualties of war.

The physical impact of the some of the above experiences can be profound, and UNICEF (1993) have conceptualized the extent of the impact as follows. They use the term 'psychosocial' to encapsulate emotional, psychological and social dimensions of well-being and identify three levels of psychosocial need:

- *discomforting psychosocial needs* – for instance, bed-wetting or not wishing to be alone, which are minimal and usually rectified through the re-establishment of everyday social interaction;
- *disturbing psychosocial needs* – for instance, manifest through depression or sleep disturbance, when some type of special intervention is required;
- *disabling psychosocial needs* – for instance, inability to control emotions, such as uncontrolled anger or extreme withdrawal, that may be long-term unless highly focused 'extraordinary' intervention is implemented.

The point is that the majority of children will recover from the extreme events of conflict. They are affected at the first level and far more rarely at the second or third levels. However, recovery is speeded through strengthening the family and community, and by the restoration of order and routine. Re-establishing opportunities for play and education are key ways of healing, both for the individual and the community.

War and conflict are extreme situations, which will require an extreme response from all involved. For many children and adults, however horrific or awful their experiences, the relief created by the end of war and conflict, through either reaching a place of safety or through the cessation of hostilities, will be sufficient to enable them to regain psychological balance and not to be permanently damaged by the psychological impact of their experiences.

Factors affecting the impact of violence

Children will manifest stress dependent on the extent, nature and severity of their experiences. The most common circumstance is that it is a series of events, not just violence itself, which will have an impact on the child and their community. There are other variables such as age, gender and culture that researchers have explored in an attempt to quantify the effect of violence. We will now consider some of these findings.

Services and other provisions which are taken for granted during peacetime, such as schools, jobs, banks, power supplies and so on, do not function in war. Difficult and adverse situations that people over-come in everyday life become exacerbated because of war and unrest with an inevitable impact on children. Opportunities for play and the everyday experiences of childhood are lost. Therefore, when consider-ing the experiences of a group of Afghani child refugees, UNICEF notes that psychosocial stresses include a 'long, hot rainy season with poor sanitation and insufficient drinking water; lack of educational opportunity; separation from important people', and family stresses such as depression and unemployment (UNICEF 1993: 185). UNICEF researchers concluded that children's responses to stressful experi-ences will be largely determined by cultural expectations. Added to this, the nature and severity of events will also have an effect on children's responses. In addition, the frequency and number of extreme experiences will also be a factor.

Pynoos and Nader (1993), researching into the psychological well-being of women and children after traumatic events, noted that those who had been subject to multiple traumatic experiences had the most difficulties with everyday life, and that the more traumatic the events experienced by children, the higher the stress-related behaviour.

A range of other factors are important when noting the impact of armed conflict on children. To mention a few, perception of threat is important, and from a child's perspective the threat of being separated from loved ones is more frightening than threats to physical safety. Another important factor is whether the child perceives themselves to be a victim because they were targeted individually as opposed to being a witness. The argument here is that if a child feels that they are a victim by accident, then they are better able to reconcile themselves to this than the feeling that they have been singled out personally for attack.

Age and gender are considered to be important determinants of the ability of children to cope with the traumas of war. Researchers provide conflicting information about the exact attribution of age and gender to the severity of the experience of the traumas of war and conflict. Elbedour *et al.* (1993: 809) cite Rutter (1981) who reports that children aged 6 months to 4 years were most affected. They also quote Bowlby (1969) who concludes that children between 6 months and 6 years face the greatest risk of developing psychopathology during trauma. Other researchers (e.g. Kinston and Rosser 1974) have found that school-aged children from the age of 8 onwards are most likely to experience psychological damage after trauma.

Interestingly, the results relating to gender are clearer: in general it would appear that girls are more able to cope with traumatic stress than boys.

Resolution through play

Research has also pointed to the importance of 'psychological resolution' for a child. An 'appropriate understanding of experiences seems to be an essential component of well-being for all children . . . making sense of the experience helps empower the individual' (UNICEF 1993:185). UNICEF also stress that, while therapy and counselling are important tools and culturally relevant in many communities, of more importance is the need to strengthen the family to support the child's recovery by supporting families to function and rebuild a community. This means that a range of normal experiences are restored, from opportunities to play to those of forming friendships within a secure social network.

Case study

The importance of strengthening families and rebuilding communities was at the heart of initiatives by a number of aid agencies in the Balkans to establish early childhood centres as an emergency response. Centres were provided in refugee camps and were established in areas hit by conflict.

The reasons for doing this included the need to provide opportunities for families and communities to focus on the future, as well as the wish to ensure that children's development was not interrupted. The provision of basic early childhood activities acted as a focus for adults in the community, who were able to be involved as volunteers working in the centres. This was reported as an empowering and positive experience.

At the same time children had opportunities to play in an atmosphere that was supportive and reinforcing of normality in the face of the unpredictability of the surrounding conflict.

In some cases, resources were provided to enhance activities that had been established by members of the community during months of conflict. In one area of the Balkans, teachers and parents had worked together to set up makeshift early childhood centres in the basements of their apartment blocks.

During months of shelling and fighting, parents carried on creating structured opportunities for young children to play. When the fighting reduced and aid agencies arrived, parents were able to carry on providing activities and felt in retrospect that the provision of early childhood activities during these extreme events had been enormously beneficial to both adults and children.

(Hyder, unpublished notes)

Sheila Melzak (1995: 116) writes about the enormous losses experienced by refugee children, affecting the progress of their development:

The detail of the developmental process and expectations on children of the society varies across cultures e.g. the balance between play and work during childhood varies across cultures. In fact in all cultures research shows that children will spend their time during their play imitating the activities of adults in their community and exploring various aspects of adult social roles. As well as the usual domestic and work roles, refugee children may have seen adults they knew as violent soldiers, as humiliated victims, as rescuers, as bystanders – helpless or active.

Other researchers have noted that the impact of war, if not addressed, can reach down into future generations. For instance, when writing about Holocaust survivors Danieli (1958), cited in Elbedour *et al.* (1993: 808), states that children of such survivors 'seem to have consciously and unconsciously absorbed their parents' Holocaust experiences into their lives in toto. Many children manifest Holocaust-derived behaviours particularly on the anniversaries of their parents' traumata'.

Elbedour *et al.* (1993: 808) go on to describe the work of Rosenthal and Rosenthal (1980: 578) who treated a 7-year-old girl whose grandparents had survived a concentration camp. They quote the girl as follows: 'My fears come from my grandfather to my father, from my father to myself. I am the stop-sign'.

Healing and play

Freud thought that emotional trauma experienced at an early age would return to haunt the child at a later age: 'What children have experienced at the age of two and have not understood; at some later time it will break into their lives with obsessional impulses; it will govern their actions'. This means that children will live in expectation of an unexplored trauma. In addition, 'if the child victims do not succumb to emotional illness in the immediate post war years, it is still possible they will be stricken years later' (Galante and Foa 1968 quoted in Ellebedour *et al.* 1993: 808).

Freud believed that play is a means by which children express their innermost conflicts and desires. Through psychoanalytic therapy a child can play with toys, providing a metaphorical insight into their world. In this way the therapist can understand, integrate and communicate the meaning of the child's play to the child in order to promote resolution.

Psychoanalytic theory is an underpinning foundation of a consideration of PTSD. As Pynoos and Nader (1993: 536) note, 'Freud's original model of traumatic helplessness defines trauma as one where "external and internal, real and instinctual dangers converge".' Pynoos and Nader (1993: 535) have written about the concept of post-traumatic stress in children. They note that:

> Like adults, children respond to trauma with symptoms of re-experiencing, emotional constriction or avoidance, and increased arousal ... The re-experiencing of traumatic phenomena is evidenced by traumatic play, behavioural enactments, intrusive thoughts, images, sounds or smells, traumatic dreams, and psychological reactivity reminders.

They go on to argue that children will avoid triggers such as places or objects that remind them of past events. However, this type of behaviour may also lead to a loss of interest and enjoyment or even a loss of skills in other areas of life. What Pynoos and Nader describe as 'traumatic avoidance' will result in interference in everyday functioning. It can be argued, if this is the case, that one of the restorative functions of play is to enable children to return to past events in play and to regain control over those events and so reach some resolution.

Young children may be partially protected from the impact of a traumatic event as they do not fully perceive or apprehend the full extent of the danger of the situation. As has already been noted, research findings indicate that children's responses are mediated by the responses of the adults around them. When adults try to minimize real threats, children can become confused, and learn not to trust adults, but they very quickly use their own assessment of the potential threat of danger. Therefore there is a fine balance between not alarming children and not misleading them about the seriousness of a situation.

Drawing on academic and clinical research from conflict situations and traumatic events around the world, Pynoos and Nader (1993: 536) describe how young children 'may desperately envision the need for outside help while invoking fantasies of superhuman powers primarily to protect themselves and their physical integrity against attack. School-aged children may entertain conscious fantasies of intervening, for example, taking the gun out of the assailant's hand'. As we will see later on, it is important that we support this type of play.

Play and recovery

There is an interesting link drawn between children's denial of events (in psychoanalytic terms) and play. Denial in its original usage did not mean disavowal of reality; indeed, in Anna Freud's original description (1936) it was a method that children especially employed to mitigate 'objective pain; by use of fantasy or imagined action' (p. 536). This suggests that children's ability to play and change events, integrating fantasy and reality, is in fact a valuable and important coping mechanism.

When children are stuck

While so far we have noted the restorative and healing nature of play, for those children seriously affected by trauma, it is argued by some that play may not be healing unless supported and guided: 'Traumatic play includes the redramatisation in play of episodes of the event or the repetition of play in traumatic themes'.

Terr (1981) observed that if children's traumatic play fails to provide relief, it may aggravate rather that soothe the condition, and often ends unsatisfactorily, in contrast to normal play. This is because in play, children are not simply repeating an action but are manipulating the object or event as well, sometimes towards a more positive outcome. Therefore, adults have a role in supporting and sometimes moving on, in a sensitive fashion, children's play scripts.

In these situations it is important that practitioners are alert to signs that a child is experiencing difficulties, and understand when and how to intervene to move play on. Moreover, it is important to know when and to whom a child can be referred in order to help them move on and reconcile themselves to any emotional difficulty that cannot be resolved in the setting through play.

What are the signs that a child is experiencing difficulty? Again it is hard to draw out generalized signs. However, very fixed play patterns that do not develop and extend over time may be one sign, as may over-aggressive reactions that are sustained over time.

If a child is newly-arrived in a group, is, perhaps, unable to communicate in English and is unused to the routines and expectations of an early years setting it is hard to assess if they are experiencing difficulties. Therefore, it is important to build up a picture of a child over time, based on establishing a good relationship not just with the child but also with their carers. In this way any behaviour that causes concern can also be discussed with parents and then an informed decision can be made as to whether or not the child needs additional help.

An important point to bear in mind is that:

> there is not an automatic relationship between psychological damage and a child's experience of extreme events. Various mediating factors such as meaning, continuity of parenting, and community cohesion act between the potentially traumatic experiences and their subsequent effects. Also, refugee children may show extreme behaviour that does not have the same meaning as that of children showing the same extreme behaviour with a different history.
>
> (Melzak 1995:120)

Conclusion

In conclusion, this chapter has drawn on some of the research in the field of children and armed conflict and has shown that many children have emotional and behavioural reactions to extreme events. For young children, the primary caregivers have a role in protecting them by maintaining a sense of safety and certainty. Nevertheless, younger children may feel responsible or may blame their parents and carers for the catastrophic events they have experienced.

Children's reactions to violence may be visible in their feelings and play behaviours long after reaching a place of safety – they do *not* forget. It is through play that children recreate but also come to terms with their experiences, and opportunities for play are also healing for the wider community.

4

WHAT WORKS: FIRST PRINCIPLES TO PROMOTE PLAY

I remember when R first started at the playgroup. He was just three and had arrived recently from Eritrea. He was so angry and frustrated he threw things around and hit other children.

Over the weeks he began to trust us and start communicating with the other children. I think he really benefited from his time with us. We were a place of safety.

When S, a four year old Kurdish girl from Turkey, arrived she also wouldn't communicate, wouldn't play, and for many weeks refused to be physically separated from her mother. It took a long time before she felt able to join in with activities and begin to work out some of her anxieties through play.

(Hyder 1998: 93)

This chapter sets out useful concepts and those first principles that underpin good practice when supporting and encouraging play in early years settings, with young asylum-seekers and with refugees. It highlights the issues early years practitioners need to be aware of and sets the scene for Chapter 5 which concentrates in more detail on good practice and outlines some specific play activities with young asylum-seeking and refugee children.

As well as discussing the principles of good early years practice for children who have experienced war and armed conflict, this chapter will consider the concept of resilience, followed by discussion of the importance of communication with parents and families, and with children. Finally the role of anti-racism and good inclusive practice will be outlined.

Play as a first principle   ■

As has already been set out in earlier chapters, play offers children important ways of making sense of their experiences. Play in itself is a healing process which gives children an opportunity to 'play out' their feelings and problems. Early years settings can provide children with valuable opportunities to play and explore, so enabling them to come to terms with past events.

These play opportunities include both adult-led activities with an anticipated outcome that are exploratory, and those opportunities for free-flow play that are imaginative and open-ended.

Evidence suggests that in many cases young children who have experienced the trauma of conflict or displacement do not need specialized therapy or intervention. The majority of children who are manifesting distressed behaviours will, after just a short time in an early years group, begin to benefit from the relationships, routine, surroundings and materials of the setting (Tolfree 1996). Children will have a safe space and can start establishing relationships with sympathetic and supportive adults.

Frameworks for good practice   ■

It is helpful to think about the frameworks that are needed to support effective services for refugee children and their families. What is interesting to note is that the principles within such frameworks are those that form the basis of good-quality services for all children and families, not just refugees and asylum-seeking children.

A key framework for working with refugee children is known under the acronym STOP. This framework was first devised by the Swedish Save the Children organization (Gustafsson 1986). It sets out an easy to remember way to ensure that the key principles of good early years practice to support children affected by conflict are in place, and as a framework it can apply not just to the provision of early years services in an emergency situation, but once children have sought refuge. STOP stands for:

S – space and structure
T – trust, time and talking
O – opportunities to play
P – partnership with parents

Space and structure are vital to any early years programme. For a refugee child, getting to know the predictable routine of the early years setting will be an important antidote to the chaos they may have experienced. For families living in temporary housing, conditions may be cramped and children also need the physical space of the setting.

From the perspective of the young child, **trust** is often the primary casualty of war. The primary carer, often the mother, may be so affected by the enormous changes in the family's life that she is unable to meet the child's basic needs.

Time is needed to re-establish trusting relationships through **talking**, play and creative activities. Young children often feel that they have enormous power, because their feelings are so strong and overwhelming. This may, in turn, make them feel guilty or responsible for the huge changes that have befallen them and their families. By creating a place of safety and allocating time for talk and play, it is possible to explore a child's feelings and begin to explain and give meaning to events – so helping to remove feelings of guilt.

Opportunities to play are some of the defining features of childhood. These can range from organized group activities such as games, dancing and singing, to explorative play with water, clay and construction toys, and imaginative social play in the home corner and other areas.

Parents and other carers will themselves need support and opportunities to talk, or just to sit and feel safe in the setting. It is vital to welcome carers and let them participate as much or as little as they choose. It is essential to support carers' ability to care.

There are other theoretical approaches that are useful to bear in mind when designing services that best meet the needs of refugee and asylum-seeking children. For instance, the notions of risk and resilience are very important concepts to consider.

Seeing the whole child – risk and resilience

There is an established body of research that sets out to explain why some children survive and thrive following events that others find it hard to cope with. These theories of risk and resilience have been elaborated over the years (Rutter 1985). Evidence suggests that younger children are more resilient than older children, although there are some exceptions.

For instance, children under the age of 5 who had lived through a natural disaster were found to be more affected than older children (Rutter 1985). However, the main point is that while young children are affected by disaster, they are also more likely to respond to the supportive environment and relationships of an early years setting, and to play opportunities as healing experiences.

What is resilience?

Very simply, in relation to human development, resilience is the capacity to cope with life and adapt to change. It is a combination of factors, based on the synergy between the individual and their environment, that will affect the capacity to survive and develop.

Protective factors that promote resilience for asylum-seeking and refugee children include:

- previous experience of good parenting;
- carers who can respond to the child's current emotional needs;
- being able to express feelings and anxieties to someone who listens and reflects in a way appropriate to the child's development;
- opportunities for self-expression through imaginative and multi-sensory play, games and artistic expression;
- a positive early years or school environment that provides appropriate play and learning opportunities, friendly peers and experiences of pleasure and success;
- opportunities to maintain and value the family's language and culture.

Other factors within the individual child include good health, a positive disposition and stability.

Adverse factors that increase risk for asylum-seeking and refugee children include:

- experience of separation or loss;
- family secrets about disappearances or deaths;
- frightening experiences of violence;
- unfamiliar carers or those unable to create a supportive environment;
- family tensions related to parents' experiences;
- poor housing and lack of access to basic welfare services;
- few opportunities for unsupported play;
- racism and hostility.

In a young child, adverse factors may include general health, a mental or physical disability and temperament – including for instance an infant who is hard to console.

What Michael Rutter (1985) and others (see Mental Health

Foundation 1999) have noted is that adverse or risk factors are cumulative. Most children can cope with the experience of one or even two of the risk factors listed above – it is when there are four or more in place that children are less likely to cope.

However, the risk factors have to be set against the factors that promote resilience. Therefore, the more factors to promote resilience that are in place the more able a child is to deal with adversity. The important point to note is that adversity or resilience factors are not just personal attributes or traits – environmental and social conditions will also bolster or harm a child.

Early years services can contribute to combating the risk factors and maximizing the protective factors by providing a safe and predictable environment within which to build relationships. Early years settings and services also provide safe and structured opportunities for play, which is one of the most healing experiences for children who have encountered war and conflict. Evidence from war zones and areas of conflict around the world has shown that children will in many cases overcome trauma and benefit from opportunities to be together and play, even if just for a few hours a day (Tolfree 1996).

First principles to promote play – what do children need in order to play?

Supportive adults

When adults are themselves stressed the enthusiasm and joy of children's play can be hard to bear. Children will either be in constant battle with adults or will stifle their wish to play. Adults working in early years services either as childminders, nursery workers, teachers or assistants can all bring their professional knowledge to bear to support children in play. The opportunity for physical play, development and expression is also an important right that can be denied to children affected by conflict.

Space

Life in temporary accommodation or in camps, perhaps having spent time in hiding, means that children may not have had an opportunity to learn to play, and to fully express themselves. Once in the UK families may be living in cramped temporary accommodation or in hostels where there is little space for children to play safely.

The space and resources of the early years settings will provide a vital opportunity for young children to explore and play in an unrestrained way within a structured and safe setting. Opportunities for running and jumping are limited when parents are concerned about children's safety in the outside world. The outside space in the early years setting may be the only safe playing space that some refugee children are able to use.

Materials

Children will use anything to hand for play, and will be as happy with natural materials, such as stones or water, as with the manufactured equipment found in many early years settings (Molteno 1996). Children may have been denied the opportunity to play with toys and equipment as families have had to move from place to place with few possessions in order to find a place of safety. Equally, toys may not be part of the culture of childhood within which the children have grown up. Nevertheless, materials, however simple, are important props and transformative objects for play. Early years settings can introduce children in a safe and non-threatening way to toys and equipment they may not be familiar with, but may be used extensively in educational and other provision in the UK.

Communication

Having established the clear benefits of play-based early years provision for young children, the next principle that is important to establish is that of good communication. Communication based on trust and mutual respect and understanding is at the heart of reconciliation and healing. This section will focus on communication and building relationships with adults and children as one of the key principles of effective early years practice when working with young asylum-seeking and refugee children and their families. Remember that 'if a parent is incapacitated or unavailable, other significant people in a young child's life can play an enabling role, whether they are grandparents, older siblings, family day-care providers, or nursery school teachers. In many situations, it may make better sense to strengthen such available informal ties to kin and community' (Garbarino 1992: 156).

Communicating with parents

It is a parent's first instinct to protect their child. Parents worldwide undergo enormous sacrifices to try to make a better life for their children. Normal stresses of life such as poverty, unemployment, limited or no access to healthcare and education can make parents' jobs very hard. Living in a war zone or through unremitting violence will make this work even harder.

As already described, one of the impacts of war is the loss of control felt by those most affected. Feeling out of control as a parent can be very damaging. Depression and helplessness are very common feelings reported among refugee parents. Landers (1998) reports that the impact of depression on parenting skills is particularly damaging for refugee children. Adults who are depressed will look sad and anxious and are less likely to talk, interact and respond. Depressed people are more likely to be irritable and less likely to invite and support a close, consistent relationship with their child.

This can be very serious for infants and young children who require adults to respond to and reflect in a positive way their first engagements with the world. If adults are unable to respond to and reinforce a child's first social interactions, children lose confidence and self-esteem suffers. Added to this, developmental progress is interrupted as children receive erratic and inconsistent feedback about their behaviours.

Once in the UK, these parents' feelings of helplessness may well remain, particularly given the sometimes difficult experience of being an asylum-seeker or refugee in the UK today. A very important role for any early years service is the restoration of asylum-seeking and refugee parents' beliefs in their own skills and abilities to parent. Early years services therefore have a role supporting children by providing responsive relationships, but also in working with parents to rebuild confidence and self-belief.

It is important to recognize that this role does not have to be fulfilled through the provision of counselling or any specialized service. Instead the normal relationships of the early years setting, such as the welcoming environment, daily conversations and normal requests for parental involvement and support, can be very healing for parents. In addition, opportunities for specialized classes, perhaps based on child development or English, welcome parents in with a purpose and so build self-confidence.

Play as emotional support – what families say

Lois Mutesi, a UK-based refugee from Rwanda, completed a degree in early childhood studies in 2003, including a dissertation (unpublished) which focused on how schools were meeting the emotional needs of asylum-seeking and refugee children in the foundation stage.

Lois conducted the research partly because of the reception her own child had received when starting nursery some years previously. Lois felt that the teaching staff, while well meaning, were ill-prepared and ill-informed: they found it hard to communicate with refugee parents, to welcome them properly and to explain the play-based curriculum used in the school.

For her research Lois conducted a series of interviews with parents and staff in London schools. What she found was that schools were confused about the details of the refugee communities they were working with. For instance, there was a lack of clarity about the origins and languages of some refugee families. In addition, teachers did not appear to make good induction procedures with individual families a priority. Consequently, they were not always equipped to meet the individual needs of refugee children. Lois herself also noted that she, as a new parent, was not introduced to the play-based curriculum. As a result she was at first at a loss to see its value.

When speaking to parents, she found that settings were able to provide real value where there were focused and detailed whole-school strategies in place to support and welcome refugee children and parents. These strategies included good induction, pairing children up with 'buddies' as they started in the nursery or school, and a welcome for parents with clear details about how they could become more involved in their child's education.

Added to this, Lois also noted that one way schools had found to reduce aggression and name-calling in the playground was to pair older children with younger children in the setting. This was achieved through, for instance, asking a Year 2 class to come into nursery and read with children and so form positive relationships.

Another successful strategy was to ensure that there were specific measures available to support children's emotional well-being if problematic issues did arise. Therefore, initiatives such as the 'Place2Be', which was a highly successful school-based counselling service for children, were seen to have particular value.

Lois found that parents welcomed the opportunity to come into class and help with specific activities. Further specific support which was welcomed included the provision of classes for English language and the chance to talk to staff about the curriculum. Lois also found that play was very important to support the emotional needs of refugee children. Some of the more successful schools noted how refugee children seemed to benefit from outdoor play opportunities and expressive activities such as drawing and painting.

Lois recounted, from her own experience of growing up in a refugee camp, her memories of play as a rarer experience for children, as they were expected to work from an early age to support the family. Formal education started at a later age, (6 or 7), and was very much based on rote learning.

However, when reflecting on her own childhood in the light of being a student of early childhood studies, Lois noted how much she had gained from the times when she did play. She had made her own dolls, had made their clothes and woven baskets and spent time in imaginative play. She found that this was an important experience shared with other refugee parents – as they too would remember how they played as children.

Lois notes that it is as if 'something clicks', as parents remember playing freely as children. They realize that this doesn't happen in the UK in the same way, but that early years settings and nurseries try to provide such opportunities for play as an essential foundation for all that follows.

Communicating about play

All around the world parents are keen that their children have a successful education. That interest may translate itself into an emphasis on the need for formal education through formal approaches from an early age. In many parts of the world play is seen as an unproductive and limited activity. It is important to understand parents' perspectives on play, however different they are from what many UK-based early years practitioners believe. While there is great emphasis placed on play in northern Europe and North America (the amount of research conducted into play reflects this), in many parts of the world play is seen as a much more marginal occupation of childhood, before apprenticeship into adult roles:

> In industrialised nations some form of day care or home-based care exists in which there may be a formalised curriculum. By and large, these caregiving arrangements have play objects and equipment and children are encouraged to play. By contrast in developing nations day care or crèches are still rare and parents rely on relatives or friends to provide supplemental care. In most accounts of developing societies, play occurs in children's groups but is rarely encouraged.
>
> (Roopnarine *et al.* 1994: 3)

Roopnarine *et al.* link the focus on play and the development of early years services to the growth of women's employment in industrialized countries. They propose that this focus on play is at least partly due to the need to justify placing children in centres outside the home, and do this without assuming that a focus on play is somehow more enlightened and 'advanced'. Parents with a range of educational experiences from around the world will sometimes require an explanation of the play-based approach to learning. Consequently, early years practitioners need to be able to articulate their knowledge of child development and the importance of a play-based curriculum. It is very important to be able to describe and demonstrate the benefits of play – both as an essential approach to learning but also as a child's right.

Communicating with children

Practitioners have reported that children from refugee families, on arrival in the setting, may be withdrawn and appear overwhelmed by the sights, sounds and smells of the group. Some children will simply just observe what's going on, and will be wary of some situations and people. Others will be disruptive and negative, unable to settle or take part in group activities.

Behaviour will vary, and all children will need time to adjust to the group and to begin to work through any difficult feelings. It is useful to observe and monitor children's behaviour in order to notice any patterns or particular reactions to situations, sounds and events: 'Some caregivers reported observing cases of extreme withdrawn behaviour. In one situation a child had spent the first three months of child care in the corner of the room with his bag on his back. Another spoke of children who could not tolerate touch of any description' (Sims 2000: 105).

How do practitioners communicate with children who are demonstrating such behaviours? Play provides a very important medium within which to communicate and at the same time play-based activities can be introduced as a way for children to come to terms with overwhelming feelings. Taking the example of the child described above who stayed with his bag on his back for three months, having perhaps experienced all sorts of upheaval and change before arriving in the setting it was possibly not surprising that he was staying prepared and ready to flee despite the fact that he was now in a place of safety. The imprint of his experiences will not easily disappear.

So, early years practitioners need to use all their skills of communication, including play, to create a feeling of security and safety. It is also important to work on exploration of feelings and to enable children to explore those feelings safely though play. All young children experience strong emotions, and as refugee children may have lived through particularly traumatic events, activities that enable them to explore and learn to express strong feelings in a contained context are very helpful.

How children learn to express their feelings

In general, children start to use words to describe their feelings from before the age of 2. Between the ages of 2 and 3 there is a rapid increase in the number of terms children are able to use to describe different emotions. As they get older they learn to label emotions correctly, if given support and positive feedback from alert and caring carers. At this time children also use emotional language in play. From 4 onwards they understand that the same event may generate different emotions in different people, and that feelings may persist long after the event itself is past (Kuebli 1994). It is very important that children are given feedback to help them understand their feelings and be able to name them and express them appropriately, either with words, art, movement, dance or song, among other media. If children are overwhelmed with feelings that they do not understand and feel consumed by, they will often find very extreme ways of expressing themselves. This may be through rage and aggression or withdrawal.

The three main aims of supporting and encouraging refugee children to communicate are:

- to help children express their memories, feelings and thoughts;
- to help children gain a realistic understanding of what has happened to them;
- to enable children to cope better with everyday activities (Landers 1998).

Play as communication

Play is a key way of communicating with young children. Having seen the different forms of play described in earlier chapters, what should practitioners do in order to promote play effectively?

We have already established that play is a means through which children develop social skills, empathy and reflective capacities as well as intellectual and physical abilities. Good communication as good play requires adults to be sensitive to the wishes and interests of children – it requires adults to *listen* to children. Listening effectively requires different skills and takes different forms dependent on the mode of children's communication at particular points of development. As Edenhammer and Wahlund (1990: 4) note:

> If a child's play development is to be all-round and varied, it has to occur in interaction with others. There must be somewhere to play and opportunities for play with people who can listen and comment on the child's activities. Children know how they can use adults. If there are no adults around, there are no opportunities for the child to ask questions or become curious.

Therefore, for very young infants, communication is based on the playful experiences that form part of the everyday routines of care-giving. Turn-taking exchanges established through eye contact and games such as peek-a-boo can be playful and fun. An interested, responsive adult reflecting back on the child's urge to communicate is essential. These exchanges build a child's sense of self and agency in the world.

As children grow they use their senses to investigate the world, and adults can support their early exploratory play by providing space and attention. Children start to use objects around them to represent their experiences, and this type of symbolic play is a crucial underpinning of developmental experience. Again, adults can be on hand to guide, comment upon, take part in, observe or provide props and opportunities for such play.

Children learn to connect with each other, to respond to each other's play scripts and to create fantasies and worlds that test out their experiences of the world. For a child whose developmental processes have been seriously interrupted, adults sometimes need to provide the bridge to enable the child to connect with other children and adults.

If children have experienced difficult or extreme events, the aim of adult communication should be to:

- encourage children to express their feelings;
- give children the words for their feelings;
- provide the correct information and clear, honest, appropriate explanations of events.

When to find additional support

Sometimes extra help will be needed. The presence of some of the following behaviours (adapted from Daycare Trust 1998) may indicate that a child is less able to cope and may need additional support. It is important to be aware of cultural norms regarding the expression of emotions, and to avoid misinterpreting a child's actions:

- loss of interest and energy, or being very withdrawn;
- being aggressive or feeling very angry (some refugee children copy the violence they have seen around them, other children may be unable to put their feelings into words and use violence as an outlet);
- daydreaming;
- lack of concentration and feeling very restless;
- repetitive play, drawings or intrusive thoughts about traumatic events;
- physical symptoms such as poor appetite, overeating, breathing difficulties, pains and dizziness;
- failure to thrive;
- self-injury or self-abusing behaviour;
- losing recently acquired skills, for instance the ability to keep dry at night;
- nightmares and disturbed sleep;
- crying and feeling overwhelming sadness;
- being nervous and fearful of things, such as loud noises;
- having difficulties forming relationships with other children;
- delayed or inconsistent development.

It is essential that parents and carers are involved in any decisions to seek additional support. Parents may be able to provide additional insight into children's behaviours which will help in deciding whether or not referral is the next step. Again, parents are only likely to be able to provide information if a good relationship has been established.

One local authority has two initial points of referral for early years staff with concerns about refugee children's welfare. The first service is the ethnic minority achievement service's early years advisory team. If an early years setting in the voluntary or statutory sector has any concerns about a child's progress an adviser will work with staff on a language assessment. At the same time, the special educational needs advisory service is able to advise if there appear to be issues relating to behaviour or psychological well-being. An individual plan for the child can be created to provide a framework to enable issues to be addressed. Referrals can also be made to child and adolescent mental health services.

Practitioners working in child mental health services with asylum-seeking and refugee children stress the importance of multi-agency working, such as that described above, to ensure that there is good communication that works in the best interests of the child (Davies and Webb 2000).

Sometimes, dedicated and focused action from the setting itself is all that is needed. For example, a 4-year-old Somali boy at an under 5s centre refused to participate in activities or cooperate with staff or other children. Staff were increasingly concerned at his disruptive behaviour. They decided that, rather than continue to ignore his behaviour, an approach that was clearly not working, his key worker would give him at least ten minutes' individual attention each day. It quickly became clear that the new strategy was effective, with the boy more able to join in group activities – but also that this was not a short-term intervention. The individual sessions continued for five months, consisting of play activities that were chosen by the child, over which period it emerged that the boy had witnessed the shooting of his father. With the support of dedicated, sensitive staff he was able to begin to come to terms with his experience (Hyder 1998: 95).

There may be other behavioural issues that manifest themselves. Richman (1996) notes that:

- some children will be frustrated and insecure as a result of their unfamiliarity with toys, books, routine, foods and behaviours in the setting;
- some children may exhibit extreme fear of loud noises or of groups of men or men in uniform;
- some children may appear 'overactive' or 'silly'; this poor concentration and restlessness is another way in which children manifest their feelings.

Many of these behaviours will disappear after some time in the setting, where there are opportunities for children to come to terms with their feelings through play and other activities.

Tackling discrimination ◼

Children need to feel valued and be free from discrimination. Where the registered person and staff are committed to equality they recognise that children's attitudes to others are established in the early years. They understand relevant legislation and plan to help children learn about equality and justice through their play. The provision is carefully organised and monitored to ensure that all staff and children have access to the full range of activities. Family members and staff work together and share information, for example, about cultures, home languages, play activities and children's specific needs.
(Full Day Care: Guidance to the National Standards: 41 OFSTED 2001)

There is considerable press coverage of issues of asylum. Hardly a day goes by without some mention of asylum issues, whether it is a story about individual experiences in the country or more statistics or statements from the government. The majority of press coverage is negative, and it can sometimes seem as if refugees are now scapegoats for almost everything that is wrong in the UK. It would be surprising if early years workers were not affected by this coverage.

Hence, a commitment to anti-racism has to be integral to all early years activities, including play activities, and must be central to the general ethos of any early years setting. Any negative behaviours or comments about asylum-seekers and refugees, perhaps from other parents or from other children, must be tackled immediately. At the same time it is important to work on issues of self-esteem through play.

Siraj-Blatchford and Clarke (2000: 80) write about the importance of play both as a medium of expression, and as a means of building the self-esteem of young bilingual children:

> Early childhood staff have a critical role in planning an environment which encourages children's learning through play. Staff need to be aware of providing a wide variety of opportunities for all children ... Staff need to facilitate this play by encouraging children to join in with their peers and supporting interactions without controlling them.

Training on anti-discriminatory and inclusive practice is a key element of successful strategies for countering racism and other forms of discrimination in the early years (Lane 1998). It is especially important in the light of the experiences of many refugee and asylum-seeking families in the UK.

Each setting should have policies in place to reflect commitment to equality of opportunity and anti-discriminatory practice. Policies should be constructed with the involvement of whole staff teams, managers and parents, and should be regularly reviewed. As well as stating a commitment to equity for groups who may experience discrimination with reference to appropriate legislation, a policy should also give details about how the ethos and values of the setting are demonstrated in staffing, in relationships and interactions with carers and children, and in choice of play resources and other materials.

Actions which will be taken as a consequence of discriminatory practice or comments need to be clearly spelt out. Commitment to act on the policy has to be backed up by regular review and discussion of the policy. Policies should be live documents that are easily accessible to all (see Lane 1998).

For settings aiming to develop their work with asylum-seeking and refugee children and families, training has been found to be very helpful. A number of agencies are able to offer information and insight into best practice with children and families. This can range from information about the asylum process to welfare entitlements and advice; the role of child and adolescent mental health services; the role of local agencies and multi-agency working; curriculum planning for children with English as an additional language; and a focus on healing and restorative play activities within the curriculum.

Work with young children on anti-racism is also possible through play. Louise Derman-Sparks (1989) has written about the 'anti-bias curriculum', which through play-based activities with children from 2 years onwards describes how to create opportunities to enable children to learn to appreciate difference in others and also to value themselves. The aim of this method is that children learn to feel unique and special, but not at the expense of feeling superior to others: 'Through learning about each other and appreciating their diversity, children recognise that teasing, harassing and abusing one another is unfair and hurtful' (Brown 1998: xiii).

Children themselves become activists for equality as they begin to question the discrimination and prejudice they see around them. A video aimed at practitioners in the UK highlights the principles of anti-discriminatory approaches and inclusion in early years practice (Brown 2004).

Other ways to support refugee children

Build secure relationships

At the heart of rebuilding children's belief in the world is the connection with a caregiver who knows and can see the whole child. A professional relationship with a young child is based on building an attachment that recognizes and responds to the interests and personality of the child. Play is at the heart of such a relationship.

Build upon routines

When life has been chaotic, routines can help a child regain control. When a child knows what to expect next, where to go and what to do, they begin to take control of their environment and not feel subject to whatever is forced upon them.

Build self-esteem

Young children require opportunities to see themselves and their actions reflected back in the words and reactions of others. When this happens gradually over time, children begin to build a sense of self. Again play offers the perfect opportunity within which to do this.

Sims *et al.* (2002) outline key features of good practice when supporting refugee children in an early years setting. From the responses of early years practitioners in Australia, they note the importance of the following factors: consistency in care in the setting; ensuring calmness; an anchor or key person as essential; and providing outlets for powerful emotions: 'One caregiver talked about doing painting activities with thick string that the children whacked onto paper, and punching a pillow' (2003: 107). Staff training and support were also seen as important, especially in terms of providing more information about refugee experiences, strategies for supporting children and anti-discriminatory programmes.

Conclusion

This chapter has set out the core principles that form the foundation of effective support for refugee children in the early years. The role of play as a way for children to make sense of and come to terms with experiences has been stressed. We have considered the notion of resilience, that places early years experience and play provision as a protective mechanism for refugee children.

The other underpinning principles of the need for space, time, communication and good professional and personal relationships, coupled with a commitment to tackle discrimination through play and policies, have also been discussed.

5

LESSONS FROM PRACTICE: THE ROLE OF PLAY

Much of children's learning is promoted through planned play activities. Play, according to Vygotsky, is a revolutionary activity because it involves original, creative ways of thinking in imaginative situations which in turn heighten cognitive performance. Through individual and group play children can learn and consolidate social and physical skills, share ideas, experiences and feelings, explore, experiment and create. We enrich the quality of their play and learning by providing a well-planned curriculum that effectively teaches children the skills and strategies they need, promotes problem solving and decision making, and strikes a balance between child-initiated and adult-directed activities. It is accessible to everyone and enables all children to feel self-confident, proud of themselves and their families without feeling superior or inferior to others. A project on ourselves and other people, for example, could encourage all children to talk and to draw (older ones could write) about themselves – their names, their physical features, their family, their friends, their cultural practices, their favourite foods, music, toys and games.

(Brown 1998: 50/51)

This chapter will examine curricula that promote play. It will consider good practice to support play and how different early years services, including Sure Start, respond to the play and other requirements of refugee children. It will outline a range of play activities of particular benefit to asylum-seeking and refugee children.

Curricula that promote play and good practice ▰

When considering the many forms of play as described in the earlier chapters, are there some forms of play that are more beneficial than others for children affected by war and conflict?

As has been discussed already, our understanding of what constitutes play is so broad that definitions can include exploration, games with rules, symbolic games, fantasy play and more. In addition to this, play can be a solitary activity, or with a partner or in a larger group. Adults can initiate, direct, observe or reflect and participate in many ways. So what does a well-planned curriculum for refugee children look like?

The *Birth to Three* framework published by the Department for Education and Skills (DfES 2003) offers some important points when thinking about the best approaches to planning play for all children under the age of 3. The principles underpinning *Birth to Three* place emphasis on the development of a strong child, who is a skilful communicator, a competent learner and a healthy individual. The holistic nature of young children's learning is stressed, as is the need for sensitive and responsive relationships between young children and their caregivers. Play is seen as a central means through which children explore and come to understand their worlds and their relationships.

Very young infants will explore and play with the world through their senses. Sight, smell, taste and touch are key sensory experiences and children will start to play with other people and things around them initially using their senses. Trevarthen (1979) has described how babies make determined efforts to interact and respond with the people and objects around them – if adults have enough attention to notice these efforts.

Gopnik *et al.* (1999) noted how infants are predisposed to explore and understand their environments and how this information shapes their understanding of the world. Infants learn to understand the objects around them as they are described and introduced by adults and also through their abilities to manipulate and use their senses to understand objects.

What this means is that 'the close intertwining of early development requires that play experiences can be used by the child in a range of ways. When planning play experiences, practitioners should ensure that the social and emotional aspects of play are considered as well as the physical, cognitive and linguistic aspects' (Manning-Morton and Thorp 2003: 11).

The foundation stage also offers a useful set of principles beneficial for refugee and other children. It provides a good framework for developing play-based activities for young asylum-seeking and refugee children. It states: 'Well-planned play, both indoors and out-doors, is a key way in which young children learn with enjoyment and challenge. In playing, they behave in different ways: sometimes they will describe and discuss what they are doing, sometimes they will be quiet and reflective as they play'. It also states in its basic principles of planning for learning that account must be taken of children's 'social, cultural and religious backgrounds, children of different ethnic groups including refugees and asylum seekers and children from diverse linguistic backgrounds'.

The role of the practitioner is crucial in planning and resourcing a challenging environment by supporting children's learning via planned play activity; by extending and supporting children's spontaneous play; and by extending and developing children's language and communication through play. Again, the role of play is acknowledged as central to children's learning and development. Practical examples building on the principles set out in the foundation stage are included later in the chapter.

The most important point is that the early years curriculum should offer opportunities for many types of play and learning to happen throughout the day. Therefore, intense imaginative play needs to be one element of a day that also contains opportunities for exploration, dance, drama, music and games as well as investigation of the world and time spent on developing an understanding of social and emotional relationships.

Right from the start

If you currently work with refugee populations, there are several things that you can put in place in order to support families as they arrive. An important starting point is to map local resources and sources of support and information. Useful information would include:

- lists of GPs and local health services;
- local refugee community organizations;
- lists of approved interpreters and translators;
- details of local faith groups;
- details of the local racial equality council;
- relevant voluntary sector organizations to help with welfare or immigration queries, and national organizations such as the Refugee Council;
- details of local adult education classes, especially English classes;
- details about school entry or transfer;
- details of play provision.

Information in relevant languages is very important for refugee parents who may be excluded from the usual networks. It is important to remember that more than 70 per cent of the world is bi- or multilingual. While it may be hard to find interpreters and translators proficient in every language spoken by families, there may well be language groups or some languages that are commonly understood. For instance, basic Arabic is understood by families from a range of countries, although its form varies from region to region.

Induction/settling in

Once a child arrives in your setting it is important that a full induction with the carers takes place. If possible, try to ensure that an interpreter is available; perhaps a member of staff or another parent can help if you are unable to find an approved interpreter.

The induction should attempt to cover a range of issues including the following:

- the child's preferred name and the naming system used by the family;
- age and medical history;
- special requirements;
- languages spoken and understood;
- religion;
- position in family;
- earlier play or educational experience;
- likes and dislikes in terms of play activities and foods.

It is important to try to find out about a family's history but in a sensitive and non-intrusive way. Many families will have had difficult experiences with people in authority and will want to build a relationship with you before deciding to share their stories.

It is important that parents and carers are given practical information about starting times, settling in arrangements, any charges, opportunities to join in, meetings and regular closures as well as the menu and daily routines. As much information as possible should be translated.

Some settings do not know if the families using their services are refugees, because the families may or may not choose to disclose this information. However, some knowledge of current trends in refugee arrivals (see Refugee Council website) may help you. For instance, if you know that a family is from Somalia, they are very likely to be refugees or asylum-seekers.

Make use of organizations such as the Refugee Council which can provide information about a range of countries of origin so that you have details on languages and religious customs, and some idea of the political situation from which families have fled. See Rutter (2001) and NUT (2001) for useful information.

If you find that you have families from the same country in your setting, be careful before assuming that they will have anything in common. They may well be from different sides of a conflict or from opposing political factions.

It is important to outline your approach to the curriculum, whether based on *Birth to Three* or the foundation stage. A play-based approach may not be familiar to all parents, as discussed earlier, and it is important to explain the benefits of a play-based curriculum.

Encouraging belonging through play

When children arrive it is important to help them settle and begin to feel they belong. For children who may have experienced extreme events and may be feeling strongly about separating from their parents, there are certain strategies that can help a child start to feel welcome. Children can be supported by doing the following:

- letting the child stay near physically;
- getting down to the child's level;
- encouraging the child to keep eye contact;
- knowing the child's interests;
- using what the child is interested in to help them settle;
- staying physically near, but keeping quiet as the child begins to reach out and talk with other people. (Bruce 2001: 70).

The importance of language and play

Language is an important part of culture and identity. Studies have shown that when children maintain their home language, this contributes towards their sense of self-esteem and competence.

The speech and language of young children is often extremely sensitive to their environment and emotional state. Those who have been through distressing situations may lose their speech temporarily, or may only speak within the family.

Children will begin to feel at home and valued if they see or hear their family language in the setting. Bilingual books, tapes with stories and music and dual language labels can help children feel comfortable. Children must have the chance to become fluent in their home language before they become competent in English. Non-directed play with peers is a good way to encourage this competency.

Opportunities to acquire English are best supplied within the setting or the classroom, with peers providing opportunities for interaction in English. Children new to English are likely to pick up the vocabulary of the playground or informal contact before that of any instruction.

Children may say little or nothing in English at first, but they will be observing others and gain the confidence they need to start. There will be considerable variation between learners, so it is important that practitioners are familiar with the stages of language acquisition and do not confuse them with signs of developmental delay or trauma.

It is also important to learn key words in the child's first language, particularly greetings. Let refugee children teach you and the other children some words in their home language. Others in the group can be guides or buddies to non-English speakers (Rutter and Hyder 1998).

The key worker: a guide to play

The 'key worker' system used in many early years settings ensures that a child can begin to establish a close and trusting relationship with one person. This is particularly important for refugee children, who may have lost many of the significant adults in their lives. Through the creation of a safe and secure relationship, key workers can help children explore through play.

Tina Bruce (2001) writes about the importance of adults as a catalyst for children's free-flow play. Adults can take part in a number of ways:

- *by supporting the child's play agenda* – where the adult participates in the play, joins in and acts out a role;
- *through verbal guidance* – when the adult makes comments and reminds children about the storyline or points out interesting avenues;
- *participation in storylines* – by helping children to act out familiar stories;
- *creating imaginative play with props* – by using puppets or guided imagery.

As children arrive in the group it is often best to observe play and to indicate to children that you are ready to take your lead from them. Sims (2000: 7) describes how one caregiver used a strategy whereby she found one toy that the child enjoyed, and made a point of playing with that toy near the child as often as possible, encouraging the child to join her. Any play together was initially focused on the toy. She found that spending enjoyable time together (although initially solely toy-focused) gradually evolved into a trusting relationship. She emphasized that this change took a long time but rated it as a very effective strategy.

Tackling racism, supporting identity and valuing diversity through play

Maintenance of cultural links and identity is important to all children. Refugee children need to be grounded in their first language and culture, to see being Somali, Afghani or Kurdish as something to be proud of. Cultural identity is typically established by the age of 5 for people operating, as refugees are, in more than one culture. There are three important aspects of 'cross-cultural competence'. These are self-awareness, knowledge of information specific to each culture and skills which enable the individual to engage in each culture. Children are particularly skilled at operating in more than one culture and in using language appropriate to a specific setting. They may acquire English and an understanding of UK culture far faster than their parents and carers. However, as mentioned previously, refugee parents, unlike other migrants, may place particular stress on children maintaining cultural identity and adhering to tradition because such families often hope to return once the political situation has changed. In some cases, families will have experienced persecution and oppression because of their identities, and therefore place even more importance on the maintenance of identity when in exile.

It can be particularly distressing for refugee parents if children appear to be uninterested in, or even worse to be positively rejecting, their language and identity. It is important that even young children are supported to maintain their cultural connections. This may mean ensuring that children's play experiences incorporate, where possible, the stories, folk tales, games and music of the community.

Children from refugee and asylum-seeking families need to see play resources that reflect a range of family groups. For example, a mother and her children, or children living with grandparents. Children also need to see other children enjoying translated folk tales, or dancing to music that is a family favourite. This will contribute to the feeling that they are accepted, have something to offer and that home is not something to be ashamed of. As part of this process, books, posters, puzzles, games and toys must be evaluated for messages about diversity to ensure they contain positive, realistic and accurate images that are not stereotyped or exotic (Lane 1998).

Research has shown that children as young as 2 or 3 are aware of difference and begin to develop positive and negative feelings about difference (Brown 1998). It is important that early years practitioners support children to notice similarities and differences in the way children and adults look, speak and dress in their family groups and to see difference as positive. Unless work is done by early years educators on valuing diversity from the start, children will absorb the implicit and explicit messages about what is supposed to be 'normal' in society.

Resources for play

There are many ways to support diversity in the early years setting through the provision of a range of play resources and activities. Home corners are a vital and adaptable part of any early years setting. As well as reflecting a variety of homes, home corners can be transformed into airports, hospitals or launderettes. They offer opportunities for children to act out situations they have experienced (e.g. arriving in the UK at the airport) and/or are currently experiencing that are new and strange (e.g. using a launderette).

In addition they can also reflect the way things are done at home. Many settings already use a range of cooking and eating utensils such as chopsticks and pots to make tea. Other props are also useful. Model food can be made from clay or Playdough or bought from educational suppliers. All offer a useful starting point for children and staff. There are many other examples.

A range of realistic-looking plastic breads from around the world presents early years workers with the basis of an exciting theme and is an important adition to the home corner. Models of *injera* from Ethiopia and Chinese steamed buns as well as rye, white and wholewheat bread provide opportunities for children to say to each other, 'My family eats this'. Making the real thing is the next step, and this provides children with the chance to smell, taste and be involved in food preparation.

Home corners without the usual miniature tables and chairs offer children the chance to sit on the floor or on low stools and to take tea, eat and talk as they have seen their parents and grandparents do.

Home corners can be hung with inexpensive decorative cloth that is familiar and attractive, while a wide range of dressing-up clothes can be provided with a stress on everyday clothes from a range of communities. It is important that dressing-up clothes are not just exotic, but represent a realistic range of styles from different communities as well as allowing children a way to take on roles and develop imaginative play skills. Clothes can be bought from suppliers or made, a role that may offer refugee parents a chance to get involved.

Music and dance are also enjoyed by all children and offer opportunities for expression regardless of language skills. Very young children below the age of 2 may respond to music from the home environment. A collection of music from different countries will reassure children, particularly when they are settling in to the centre. A wide range of instruments allows children to experiment and play (Hyder 1998).

Play-based activities

In one early years centre, a brother and sister dived under the table every time they heard loud noises or planes overhead. They had recently arrived from a refugee camp. Staff discovered that this was because of an incident when the family were under attack, and to reduce this fear devised a series of activities around the theme of feelings, using stories, puppet shows, music, dance and discussion as well as painting, model-making and imaginative play. Without introducing specific information about being pursued or shot at, or about bombs or shelling, which might have been distressing, the opportunity was offered to talk in small groups about 'what scares me', 'what makes me happy', 'what do I feel like if someone shouts at me or calls me names'.

(Hyder 1998: 97)

This section will consider some examples of play activities that may be of particular benefit for young refugee children.

Diana Brandenburger (2001), an art therapist who works with refugee children and early years practitioners, suggests some activities that could be beneficial. Free, undirected activities using sand, water, clay or 'gloop' are tactile and healing. No end product is required and the exploratory and creative opportunities mean that children can safely explore the properties and potential of the materials without feeling any pressure to create an end product. Children new to English can play alongside English-speaking peers and so start to hear English informally.

Mask-making and role-play are also very positive experiences for young children who have undergone extreme situations. They provide safe, structured opportunities within which to explore anger, rage or hatred or other powerful feelings. Good and evil, power and powerlessness can also be explored safely in drama and focused role-play.

Persona dolls

Another activity that can be used to introduce the experience of being a refugee into the early years setting is a persona doll (Brown 2001). This is an almost child-sized doll that arrives in an early years group with a story to share and problems to solve. Adults introduce the doll giving his or her biography.

Starting with simple information about family and favourite activities, adults can introduce more complex issues, such as discrimination or exile, for children to reflect upon and discuss. Situations such as the birth of a new sibling, going to the dentist, death and separation can be introduced naturally and safely.

Young children invariably respond positively to the doll and can empathize with it. One way such dolls have been used is when a new child, perhaps a refugee or asylum-seeker, is about to join the group. A doll with the persona of a newly-arrived refugee can tell its story and the children in the group can begin to think about what those experiences of fighting and constantly moving and arriving in a new country must be like, and can think together about how best to welcome their new friend. Brown (2001) notes that sessions with persona dolls are very empowering for children as they are giving their own perspectives while trying to understand the world from someone else's point of view.

Story boxes

Story boxes build on the idea of story props and have been developed by Helen Bromley (2000). A story box is a shoebox equipped with props. Children are able to create 'small worlds' using whatever materials are available. Bromley proposed that children be enabled to make their own boxes – drawing on whatever material they choose – and so be enabled to tell their own stories.

Boxes can be given to children already partly equipped, and children can either develop their own stories or work in groups. The box can be decorated with a particular scenario – for instance, it could be a beach with shells and sand or a launderette with model washing machines made out of matchboxes. They are used as prompts to encourage storytelling and are a good catalyst for literacy, communication and play.

In one school, with a high number of refugee children, a teacher decided to create a story box that contained camouflage and two tanks. A young Kosovan child in the class really responded to the props. She told the story of tanks coming to her village and also produced a range of other materials in response to the box, including drawings and a poem.

Multi-sensory play

Sarah Potts (2003) describes the benefits of multi-sensory play for a Year 1 class with a significant number of refugee children. A multi-sensory curriculum is one that operates with reference to a range of learning styles (visual, auditory and kinaesthetic). It aims to provide 'first-hand experiences and learning in a sensory environment' (Potts 2003: 26).

Lights and visual resources are used to label, display and signpost (e.g. lights in the shape of a letter for visual learners); music and rhyme are used for auditory learners to access all areas of the curriculum; and kinaesthetic learners are supported through a sensory and tactile environment. There is an emphasis on learning outside, using everyday outdoor equipment such as hoops, bikes, chalk, paint, skittles to teach across the curriculum. Multi-sensory play requires planning and preparation to deliver the curriculum in an active and participative way. Therefore, imaginative application of a range of materials and props such as dressing-up clothes, carpet tiles with numbers, small world materials will enable curriculum goals to be realized.

The multi-sensory approach requires an assessment of children's learning styles and is appropriate for children with a range of styles – it is especially appropriate for kinaesthetic learners. Sarah Potts (2003: 27) notes that:

> The development of traditional Foundation materials and provision in Year One, eg the role-play area, small-world area and construction areas, sand and water trays, proves to be of particular benefit to refugee children and children at the initial stages of English.
>
> Many refugee children in Year One are not only new to UK school but to any schools as most countries do not offer formal education until the ages of 6–7. Areas which allow for

increased opportunities to interact with other children in a non-threatening environment not only help to alleviate some initial anxieties but also introduce the children to everyday English in a meaningful way.

Listening to refugee children

By creating opportunities for young refugee children to relive or reflect on past experiences through play, adults may find themselves confronted by horrific, arduous or extremely sad stories. How should an early years worker respond to such revelations, given the fact that this may be a new experience and one for which they are not fully prepared?

The main point is that it is vital to let stories emerge naturally, when a child is ready. Never force children to disclose their experiences through play, but equally do not try to shut off to what they are telling you:

> When adults play with children and listen to their stories, it is important that the comments the adults make are connected to the story, rather than to the child's reality. Many story themes express the terrible pain of loss and rejection, and it is only within the safety of the story that the child is able to express how he or she feels.
>
> (Cattanach 2001: 71)

Cattanach also alerts us to the fact that children establish play frames before engaging in imaginative play. What this means is that children signal that they are about to pretend, often through gesture or smiling and laughing. Cattanach notes that when engaged in play, children are operating at two levels, with full awareness of meanings and relationships in both the pretend and real worlds. Children are also adept at moving between their worlds in a way that adults sometimes find hard to follow.

The implication for the early years practitioner is that observation is crucial – children will reveal a great deal in their fantasy and imaginative pretend play, sometimes provoked through the use of props and resources and sometimes not. Knowing when and how to intervene comes through listening and understanding, and appreciating children's stories.

Conclusion

This chapter has considered how current curriculum frameworks offer an excellent starting point to promote play with refugee children from infancy to the end of the foundation stage. The practical actions that need to be in place to support refugee families as they arrive and settle their children in an early years setting have also been discussed. The creation of warm, supportive, responsive relationships between children and practitioners and the importance of adults sensitively joining children's play agendas has been stressed.

We have considered how play can promote diversity and self-esteem and some examples of play-based activities that may be particularly effective when working with young refugee children. The importance of listening to children and understanding all their ways and means of communication has also been emphasized.

6

WAR AND VIOLENCE IN THE WIDER WORLD: ISSUES AFFECTING PLAY

Children are able to deal with complex psychological difficulties through play. It helps them to integrate the experience of pain, fear, and loss. They wrestle with concepts of good and evil and express ideas for which they have no meaning. Children who live in dangerous environments play 'the dangerous environment'. The child can take control of an event by playing different roles and altering the outcome. In symbolic play children bridge the gap between reality and fantasy.

(Landers 1998: 38)

This chapter aims to examine some of the wider issues surrounding the rights of young asylum-seeking and refugee children to play. Particular issues that will be focused on include attitudes towards gun and superhero play, the impact on adults of working with refugee children and wider evidence of the restorative nature of play.

Gun play

Practitioners may experience a dilemma when faced with young asylum-seeking and refugee children who, in their play, appear to be acting out scenes of violence. This creates a tension for many practitioners who feel strongly that violence in the wider society, especially violence towards women, could be diminished if young boys were supported to find alternatives to violent play themes. Now, they may be faced with a group of children, boys *and* girls, who appear to benefit from the opportunity to re-enact violent situations and so experience the healing afforded through the opportunity to play out these scenes.

Sims *et al.* (2002: 106) note in their research on supporting refugee children in early years settings in Australia that:

> Most caregivers attempted to redirect gun and knife play. One caregiver explained how she had once worked with a child to turn the gun the child had built into a helicopter. Another talked with groups of children who had regularly engaged in violent chasing games about alternative strategies they could use to catch people. Many services operated a gun-free environment, so children who brought these toys from home were gently asked to leave them in their bags. One caregiver felt that acknowledging children's anger was important, as was listening and demonstrating understanding.

Penny Holland (2003), in her work on war, weapon and superhero play, reviews the literature on the links between gun play, superhero play and aggressive behaviour in children, especially boys: 'I have challenged the view that we can draw a simple connection between war, weapon and superhero play and aggression' (p. 14). In reviewing the available evidence, Holland concludes that parental attitudes to violence and the practice of physical punishment in the home are stronger predictors of non-pretend aggressive behaviour in boys. Added to this, practices of 'zero tolerance' towards pretend gun play, superhero fighting and so on may be counter-productive in that these prohibitions restrict opportunities, for boys especially, to develop imaginative play scripts.

Popular culture as depicted on television, in comics, in traditional stories and myths and legends from around the world is full of images of the superhero who asserts his or her powers through vanquishing evil, often through the use of aggression. Many boys respond to these stories by weaving such themes into their play. Boys appear to benefit from the support of imaginative play with a superhero theme, possibly involving the use of make-believe weapons, whether swords or laser guns.

From discussion with practitioners, Holland concludes that boys are better able to develop imaginative play on other themes if they are allowed to indulge in superhero-type play. They will also develop technological skills as they make play-props to support their play and will enhance their skills of socialization through being enabled to engage in superhero play.

Other reported benefits are also of interest to those practitioners with an interest in supporting asylum-seeking and refugee children. Holland draws on the work of Broadhead to emphasize the potential of superhero play as a means to develop friendships. In particular

Broadhead (1992: 48 reported in Holland 2003: 71) notes that children with English as an additional language are able to access a superhero play theme and so join in with their peers. In addition, Holland (2003: 70) quotes a practitioner as follows:

> I think one of the most useful things about superhero play is that it can be very, very simple – just chasing. And that means that children who feel totally insecure can be part of that . . . when they are admitted that can be the first game. That seems to be quite crucial. They're watching it on the tele and they see other people playing and all they've got to do is put a cloak on.

What conclusions can be drawn from the above about how practitioners may choose to respond to the violent play themes that some asylum-seeking and refugee children engage in?

Initially it seems important to disentangle why different groups of children engage in weapon and superhero play. For the majority of the children described above, weapon and superhero play may be deemed to be an exploration of what it means to be male. Their play is clearly pretend and does not seem to lead to an increase in real incidents of aggression, although the evidence here is not conclusive (see Holland 2003). Furthermore, despite concerns about being seen to encourage violent interaction – even if in play – there may well be benefits for boys as this type of play acts as a catalyst for other areas of development.

For those children who have been exposed to acts of real violence, whether as witnesses or victims, in the home or in a war zone, acting out scenes of violence through play can be seen to be more than an exploration of identity – it represents a need to come to terms with extreme experiences.

Arguably, this presents an even stronger case for a review of a 'zero tolerance' approach to weapon and war play. At the same time we need to consider what issues need to be addressed when children who are playing with violent themes for exploration purposes are doing so with children who are playing for resolution because of past experiences. Is there a need for concern when one group of children who appear to be engaged in a process of exploration are confronted with children for whom the themes of weapons and war really do have life or death implications?

In other words, is there a danger that the extreme experiences of one group of children and their need to re-enact and come to terms with their feelings may somehow 'contaminate' the play of others? The guidelines offered by Holland are useful in this respect. There need to be clear boundaries between what is real and what is pretend.

Adults must intervene if the script changes in a way that is negative, and also need to be on hand to extend the play imaginatively to ensure children gain the full benefit.

Other questions also emerge. For instance, is it acceptable to allow one group of children to engage in such play, because of their earlier experiences, and at the same time stop others from exploring such themes? Practitioners report that it can be highly confusing for refugee children (especially boys) to witness and attempt to join the play of others when that play has a gun or weapons theme.

So what is the answer? Do settings where play with weapons, guns or superhero themes is supported potentially provide a more healing environment for refugee and asylum-seeking children? It is perhaps useful to refer to Penny Holland again. She concludes that it is hard to measure the benefits of relaxing zero tolerance of war, weapon and superhero play but the fact that practitioners begin to reflect on the impact of such a ban and to consider the individual interests and experiences of the children they work with is in itself beneficial.

On the other hand, the work of Dunn and Hughes (2001: 502) indicates that by the age of 6, those children who at the age of 4 had 'an interest in violent play themes demonstrated less socially developed behaviour including their ability to show empathy'. Nevertheless, the implication here as noted by Holland (2003: 39) is that there 'is not a causal connection between violent fantasy play and aggressive behaviour but rather . . . imaginative development through fantasy play may be implicated in successful social development and conflict resolution'.

What this means in practice is that practitioners need to do more than just provide a safe space and encouragement for children to develop play themes on whatever issues they choose. They must also promote and extend children's opportunities for imaginative and fantasy play. As a result, if issues of violence are explored fully and children, whatever their life experiences, feel that they have been able to play, they may be able to move on and explore new themes, and so develop their fantasy play repertoire.

War, conflict and violence in the news

Another important aspect of the impact of war, conflict and violence on young children in the UK is the presence of scenes of war and attack on television. Children who are not asylum-seekers or refugees are exposed almost daily to news stories about bombings, attacks and atrocities. For many children, including very young children, being a witness to scenes of war and terrorism is terrifying. As events escalate and reporting of large-scale violent events becomes an everyday occurrence, children's fears are reflected in their play and in their questions and observations.

Many have written about the reactions that young children may have to seeing extreme violence on the television. Following the events of 11 September 2001 and the destruction of the World Trade Centre, a 5-year-old child, living in London, asked her mother if there was going to be war and would the family be killed.

Clearly, events that have worldwide significance or that are particularly horrifying are often reported in great detail. Children may be appalled, stunned, overwhelmed or indifferent to these events. What differentiates these scenes from violence in films, computer games and other fictional accounts is often the reactions of adults. Young children especially will tune into events on television, not because they are aware that the violence portrayed is real as opposed to unreal, but because adults around them are focused and concerned.

An early years teacher at the time of the 11 September events reported scenes of children playing in groups in the playground, some standing still and others with their arms spread as planes running and swooping to crash into their friends. This play re-enactment was met with confusion by teachers. Some thought this type of play was negative and disrespectful behaviour to those that had been killed. Others felt, as the school had Muslim pupils, that it could be interpreted as provocative. Others expressed the view that it was important for children to be able to play out, in whatever way they felt appropriate, their reactions to the events.

Wherever the individual stands on these issues, what is important to remember is that global violence is more likely to increase than decrease and even the youngest children will react to events as they unfold. What this means in practice is that practitioners need to be alert and to have a range of strategies ready to deal with issues as they occur. The dominant subjects of this book have been asylum-seekers and refugees – but it is sometimes too easy to see the lives and experiences of these children as alien and out of the ordinary. No doubt many refugee children will have experienced and witnessed extreme violence. Nevertheless, it is worth bearing in mind that violence also impacts on all children even if only as witnesses.

Hamblen (2002) describes some of the responses young children may express if exposed to violence, even if this violence is reported on television. Children can manifest fear and increased anxiety, and be unable to concentrate. They may also become emotionally frozen – unable to react appropriately. They may experience sleep difficulties, seek adult attention and contact more frequently, and may regress.

As you will note, many of these reactions are similar to those of a child who has had direct exposure to violent events. The advice given to parents and caregivers is helpful for all those working with young children who have been exposed to violence either directly or indirectly. It includes: maintaining children's routines for sleeping and eating; maintaining a calm atmosphere in the child's presence; helping children to give simple names to big feelings; talking about events in simple terms during brief chats; and giving simple play props related to the actual trauma to a child who is trying to play out the frightening situation (e.g. a doctor's kit, a toy ambulance).

How it feels to work with refugee families

Blackwell and Melzak (2000) describe the potential response of teachers in the face of refugee children arriving in school, and this may also be relevant to early years practitioners. They state that:

> When children are unhappy or suffering, teachers want to help – to alleviate the pain, to quell the rage and anguish and to find constructive solutions to the children's problems. They are therefore likely to be perplexed and even distressed by children to whom it is extremely difficult to give something good: children whose hurt it is so difficult to reach, and whose pain is so great it is impossible to alleviate in the short term, and whose rage is so great that when it comes out it is quite uncontrollable.
>
> (p. 10)

Some early years practitioners with experience of working with asylum-seeking and refugee children and families may have such feelings. In the midst of all the complex demands of working with children and families, with increasing requirements to plan, assess and monitor it can be exceptionally difficult to find the energy to respond to a group of children whose experiences are so profound and whose behaviour may require so much attention apparently at the expense of other children.

Another issue that Blackwell and Melzak discuss is that the media portrayal of refugees can influence the way children and families are viewed in the school or setting. Over the years I have encountered a range of practitioners who have had to come to terms with difficult feelings aroused by working with asylum-seekers and refugees. These feelings can range from guilt and helplessness at not being able to put right or wipe out the experiences that the children have had to anger or annoyance at the fact that families just disappear after so much input, often as a result of decisions about asylum applications. In addition, some people are uncertain about how to react when families turn up who are not cowed or worn out by their experiences and who demand the best for their children. And, whether we like it or not, media coverage is insidious in its constant portrayal of asylum-seekers as scroungers and cheats.

All that can be said is that all of the reactions above are understandable. In the end, all early years practitioners have a responsibility to do the best for all the children they work with. Good practice is about meeting the individual needs of every child. This is the best approach when thinking about how to support young asylum-seeking children and their families.

Creating opportunities for play in the early years: the impact on the community

David Tolfree (1996) has written about the impact of war and conflict on communities and notes that from a child's perspective there are a range of activities to recreate a normal life that will 'restore playfulness' within the child. Tolfree stresses the fact that a range of therapeutic approaches such as individual psychoanalytic interventions may be suitable within one community but will not be appropriate within another. This is because the psychoanalytic approach has developed within a particular historical and social context and its focus is very much on the individual. However, many communities around the world have developed without the same focus on the individual and the personal. Within some communities there are collective rituals that provide opportunities for healing that need to be experienced by children in order to 'restore playfulness'. The main point is that countries such as those that have experienced conflict and war will not find it helpful for aid agencies to import psychosocial interventions that have no resonance in the local community. Instead, communities need to find ways to heal and restore normal life that make sense within their religious and cultural traditions.

Tolfree describes different approaches from around the world to overcoming the impacts of conflict and war. He stresses that the routes to healing the community, and the individual, will be found in the community itself. For instance, work in El Salvador is described when, in response to ongoing civil conflict, an agency initially offered counselling and psychotherapy. Eventually work shifted towards training local volunteers to offer a wide range of activities within the umbrella of 'mental health activity'. This was because it was noted that the effects of conflict were not always direct. Use of drugs and alcohol, domestic violence and child abuse, despair and hopelessness impacted greatly on the community. Social norms were violated as the normal means of social regulation and control had been eroded. The impact on children was that adults were so preoccupied that they had little time for them. In turn, children had little opportunity for play as the space, both physical and psychological, was not available. However, the agency also found that children and young people were less despairing and more able to look to the future. Hence, young adults were recruited to provide a spectrum of support activities that were agreed by the local community. There ranged from co-listening groups to awareness-raising about domestic violence and the provision of services for young children, and the community started to heal itself.

Another example, from the former Yugoslavia, is also useful as it focuses on early childhood. In 1992, a group of developmental psychologists from the University of Belgrade wanted to assess the impact of war on young children. Through interviews they discovered that children were preoccupied and even obsessed with war. This obsession was revealed in some of their activities such as drawing with extreme colours and the heavy use of black. Children also revealed their reactions to war in play. They were rigid and were unable to elaborate and extend play, and seemed stuck in recreating and reacting to situations in the past. They also revealed increased aggression in play. The children thought that war should end in 'extermination' and not resolution and reconciliation.

On closer observation the psychologists noticed that the children were unable to develop and extend play because of all their experiences and the constraints under which they were living. This was evidenced in the reactions of parents who revealed that they felt less competent, were isolated and felt a loss of individuality, personal identity and personal space.

Rather than focus on trauma, an intervention was initiated that concentrated on solutions. Psychologists convened groups, in the centres where communities lived, for adults and for children. The aim was to promote self-expression though crafts and creative activities, to promote social cohesiveness and to promote capacities and resilience rather than provide treatment.

Focus on play

One North London local authority recently reviewed its early years services, (voluntary, private and statutory) and found that despite being present in the borough there were very few refugee families in any of the early years services. The reasons appeared to be that despite the strong play ethos of the smaller voluntary sector groups, a number of factors meant that families did not use these services. These included: the small charges that were made for use; the fact that changes in council funding for these groups meant that free places could no longer be offered; the lack of practitioners from refugee or other minority ethnic communities; and the fact that free school places are available from the age of 3. Therefore, young refugee children's requirements for play as a restorative experience were not being met. Added to this, despite the fact that a play-based curriculum is used in most early years settings, within schools, the top-down pressures of assessment mean that the time and space for play is sometimes restricted.

The early years services, being aware of the numbers of refugee families in the area, have now initiated a series of activities to encourage families into early years services and are raising staff awareness of the principles needed to underpin good practice with refugee families and their children.

Strategies include holding meetings for families in the area using interpreters to explain the early years services, transition to primary school and the value of play in the early years. At the same time, in-service training courses are available for all staff working in settings, providing an overview of the experiences that many refugee families will have had and also stressing the importance of a play-based curriculum.

Once families are in a setting, advisory services are available that provide information about ways to support young newly-arrived bilingual children through a play-based curriculum. In addition, the special educational needs service acts as a bridge to access other mental health services if required, or to help structure an individual plan to meet the needs of children who may require additional input.

Sure Start services are alert to the importance of supporting refugee and asylum-seeking children. Initial guidance stresses the need for culturally appropriate services that fully support families that have experienced stress. In addition, guidance from the DfES for local authorities sets out how early years development and childcare partnerships should consider how to involve refugee families in planning and implementation of services. It also states how arrangements should be in place to 'provide asylum-seeking and refugee families with accessible information on local schools and admissions procedures and early years provision' (DfES 2000).

Conclusion

This chapter has explored the themes of gun play and the impact of violence on children in general, as well as considering issues for practitioners when working with refugee children. It has also briefly described how local services may focus on and respond to the particular circumstances faced by refugee families in order to make sure that children can benefit from opportunities to play in the early years.

7

CONCLUSION: PLAY AS A CHILD'S RIGHT

In war, children usually have little choice but to share the same horrors as their parents. As wars take on an ethnic, tribal or fratricidal cast, civilians and their children may find themselves the objects of genocidal violence. As one political commentator cynically expressed it in a 1994 radio broadcast before violence erupted in Rwanda, 'To kill the big rats, you have to kill the little rats'.

(UNICEF 1996)

For refugee children who have experienced the particular stresses of organised violence and war, the most therapeutic process is one by which they are enabled to become part of the community in which they live. For a child specifically this means finding a school situation in which they can meet their entitlement to learn, to make friends and to play.

(Melzak 1995: 117)

This book has:

- described the importance of the early years of life and the importance of early caregiving for young children's overall development;
- demonstrated the impact of war and violence on young children's development;
- considered the crucial role of play in restoring lost childhoods and as a child's right;
- outlined what practitioners can do to promote play and support refugee children and their families.

We have examined how children are affected by violence and war in many ways. Loss of familiar people and carers through death and violence, profound change as old ways of life and communities are destroyed and new lives rebuilt and trauma as children try to come to terms with past events, are all part of the refugee child's experience.

We have traced the conditions for optimal development for the child and noted how war and conflict destroy these conditions and erode children's rights, including the right to play.

The importance of the early years has been emphasized via a review of research on early brain development. This work reveals that the earliest relationships help shape children's responses and their ability to interact with the world.

So what do these multiple perspectives on play tell us about the role and importance of play in children's lives? Perhaps we can draw the following conclusions.

First, play is a universal feature of child development, and happens in all communities which enjoy safety and security, although attitudes to play and its details will vary.

Second, play is both the way that children express themselves and the means through which they resolve issues. Moreover, play is a means by which children learn and hypothesize about the world. Cultural, social, emotional, cognitive and other areas of developmental progress cannot be disentangled in this process.

Finally, as argued earlier, play has a role as an important healing experience for young children affected by war and conflict. This is not solely about play in isolation, as a process for the individual child. Play is part of the social fabric of a community and involves a dynamic learning and developmental exchange between the child and the world they inhabit. In a very real sense, play can return to the children of conflict their lost childhoods.

BIBLIOGRAPHY

Amnesty International United Kingdom (1999) *In the Firing Line: War and Children's Rights*. London: Amnesty International United Kingdom.

Axline, V. (1990) *Dibs: In Search of Self*. London: Penguin.

Bateson, G. (1972) *Steps to an Ecology of Mind*. New York: Ballantine.

Blackwell, D. and Melzak, S. (2000) *Far from the Battle but Still at War: Troubled Refugee Children in School*. London: Child Psychotherapy Trust.

Bowlby, J. (1969) *Attachment and Loss: Attachment* Vol. 1. London: Hogarth Press.

Boyden, J. and Mann, G. (2000) *Children's Risk, Resilience and Coping in Extreme Situations*, background paper to the consultation on Children in Adversity. Oxford: Department of Refugee Studies, University of Oxford.

Bracken, P.J. (1998) Hidden agendas: deconstructing post-traumatic stress disorder, in P.J. Bracken and C. Petty (eds) *Rethinking the Trauma of War*. London: Free Association Books.

Brandenburger, D. (2001) Art therapy with refugee children, in Save the Children and the Refugee Council, *In Safe Hands: A Resource and Training Pack to Support Work with Young Refugee Children*. London: Save the Children.

Broadhead, P. (1992) Play-fighting, play or fighting? – from parallel to co-operative play in the pre-school, *Early Years*, 13(1): 45–49.

Bromley, H. (2000) Lifting the lid on the magic of storytelling, in *Early years Educator* Vol 2, No 8.

Bronfenbrenner, U. (1979) *The Ecology of Human Development*. Cambridge, MA: Harvard University Press.

Brown, B. (1998) *Unlearning Discrimination in the Early Years*. Stoke-on-Trent: Trentham Books.

Brown, B. (2001) *Combating Discrimination: Persona Dolls in Action*. Stoke-on-Trent: Trentham Books.

Brown, B. (2004) *Celebrating diversity: Inclusion in practice*. London: Persona Doll Training.

Bruce, T. (1997) *Time to Play in Early Childhood Education*. London: Hodder & Stoughton.

Bruce, T. (2001) *Learning through play: Babies, Toddlers and the Foundation Years*. London: Hodder & Stoughton.

Bruner, J. (1983) *Child's Talk: Learning to use Language*. Oxford: Oxford University Press.

Burlingham, D. and Freud, A. (1942) *Young Children in Wartime*. London: Allen & Unwin.

Cattanach, A. (1994) *Play Therapy: Where the Sky Meets the Underworld*. London: Jessica Kingsley.

Cattanach, A. (2001) Play and refugee children, in Save the Children and the Refugee Council, *In Safe Hands: A Resource and Training Pack to Support Work with Young Refugee Children*. London: Save the Children.

Cohen, D. (1993) *The Development of Play*, 2nd edn. London: Routledge.

Cole, E.K.H. (2003) *A Few Families too Many: The Detention of Asylum-seeking Families in the UK*. London: Bail for Immigration Detainees.

Davies, M. and Webb, E. (2000) Promoting the psychological well-being of refugee children, *Clinical Child Psychology and Psychiatry*, 5(4): 541–54.

Daycare Trust (1995) *Reaching First Base – Meeting the Needs of Refugee Children from the Horn of Africa*. London: Daycare Trust.

Daycare Trust (1998) *Refugee Children and Childcare: A Guide to Help Childcare Staff Support Refugee Children in Childcare and Educational Services*. London: Daycare Trust.

Derman-Sparks, L. (1989) *The Anti-Bais Curriculum: Tools for Empowering Young Children*. Washington: National Association for the Education of Young Children (NAEYC).

DfES (2000) Planning Guidance for Early Years Development and Childcare Partnership Plans 2000/2001. London: DfES

DfES (2003) *Birth to Three: A Framework to support Children in their Earliest Years*. London: DfES.

Dunn, J. and Hughes, C. (2001) 'I got some swords and you're dead': violent fantasy, antisocial behaviour, friendship and moral sensibility in young children, *Child Development*, 72(2): 491–505.

Edenhammer, K. and Wahlund, C. (1990) *No Development Without Play! Methods and Conditions for Children's Play*. Stockholm: Radda Barnen.

Elbedour, S., ten Bensel, R. and Bastien, D.T. (1993) Ecological integrated model of children of war: individual and social psychology, *Child Abuse and Neglect*, 17: 803–819.

Freud, A. (1936) *The ego and mechanisms of defence*. London: Hogarth Press.

Freud, S. (1968) Inhibitions, symptoms and anxiety, in J. Strachey (ed. and trans.) *The standard edition of the complete psychological works of Sigmund Freud* (Vol. 23, pp. 3–137). London: Hogarth Press. (original work published 1939).

Golante, R. and Foa, F. (1988) An epidemiological study of psychic trauma and treatment effectiveness for children after a natural disaster. *Journal of the American Academy of Child Psychiatry*, 25(3), 357–363.

Garbarino, J., Dubrow, N., Kostelny, K. and Pardo, C. (1992) *Children in danger: Coping with the consequences of community violence*. San Francisco, CA: Jossy-Bass.

Gordon, R. and Wraith, R. (1993) Responses of children and adolescents to disaster, in J.P. Wilson and B. Raphael (eds) (1993) *International Handbook of Traumatic Stress Syndrome*. New York: Plenum Press.

Gopnik, A., Meltzoff, A. and Kuhl, P. (1999) *How Babies Think*. London: Weidenfeld & Nicolson.

Groos, K. (1901) *The Play of Man*. London: Heinemann.

Gustafsson, L.H. (1986) *The STOP Sign – A Model for Intervention to Assist Children in War*. New York: Radda Barnen.

Haight, W., Wang, X., Fung, X., Williams, K. and Mintz, J. (1999) Culture and environment, universal, developmental, and variable aspects of young children's play: a cross-cultural comparison of pretending at home, *Child Development*, 70(6): 1477.

Hall, G. S. (1908) *Adolescence*. Appleton: New York.

Hamblen, J. (2003) *PTSD in Children and Adolescents*. http://www.hiddenhurt.co.uk/Articles/PTSDkids.htm.

Holland, P. (2003) *We Don't Play with Guns Here: War, Weapons and Superhero Play in the Early Years*. Maidenhead: Open University Press.

Home Office (2003) http://www.ind.homeoffice.gov.uk/asylum.

Huizinga, J. (1949) *Homo Ludens: On the Origins of Culture in Play*. London: Routledge.

Hutt, C. (1979) Play in the under 5s: form, development and function, in N. G. Howells (ed) *Modern Perspectives in the Psychiatry of Infancy*; New York: Brunner/Marcel.

Hyder, T. (1998) Supporting refugee children in the early years, in J. Rutter and C. Jones (eds) (1998) *Refugee Education: Mapping the Field*. Stoke-on-Trent: Trentham Books.

Hyun, E. (1998) *Making Sense of Developmentally and Culturally Appropriate Practice in Early Childhood Education*. New York: Peter Lang.

Isaacs, S. (1926) *Intellectual Growth in Children*. London: Routledge.

Jambor, J. (2000) The importance of play to children's brain development, *Playrights*, XXII (1–2): 26–8.

Kinston, S. and Rosser, R. (1974) Disaster: Effects on mental and physical state. *Journal of Psychomatic Research*, 18, 437–456.

Klein, M. (1955) The Psychoanalytic Play Technique, in M. Klein, P. Heimann and R. Money-Kyrle, (1955) *New Direction in Psychoanalysis*. London: Tavistock.

Krell, R. (1990) Children who survived Japanese concentration camps: Clinical observations and therapy. *Canadian Journal of Psychiatry*, 35(2): 149–52.

Krogh, Y. and Montgomery, E. (1993) *Conceptualising anxiety in torture survivors: an investigation of children of torture survivors, Torture*, Supplementum 1.

Kuebli, J. (1994) Young children's understanding of everyday emotions, *Young Children*, 49(3).

Landers, C. (1998) *Listen to Me: Protecting the Development of Young Children in Armed Conflict*. New York: Office of Emergency Programs Working Paper Series. UNICEF

Lane, J. (1998) *Action for Racial Equality in the Early Years: Understanding the Past, Thinking About the Present, Planning for the Future: A Practical Handbook for Early Years Workers*. London: National Early Years Network.

Machel, G. (1996) *Promotion and Protection of the Rights of Children: Impact of Armed Conflict on Children*. Special Study report for the United Nations, http://www.unicef.org/graca/.

Manning-Morton, J. and Thorpe, M. (2003) *Key Times for Play: The first three years*. Maidenhead: Open University Press.

Meade, G. (2003) The brain debate, *Early Childhood Practice*, 5(2): 5–18.

Melzak, S. (1992) Secrecy, privacy, survival, repressive regimes, and growing up, *Bulletin of the Anna Freud Centre*, 15: 205.

Melzak, S. (1995) What happens to children when their parents are not there? Ouder-en kindzorg voor migranten en vluchtelingen. Van Gorcum Assen. London: Medical Foundation for the Care of Victims of Torture.

Mental Health Foundation (1999) *Bright Futures: Promoting Children's and Young People's Mental Health*. London: Mental Health Foundation.

Molteno, M. (1996) *Starting Young: Principles and Practice in Early Childhood Development*. London: Save the Children.

Mutesi, L. (2003) Healing and hearing. Unpublished dissertation for degree in early childhood studies, Roehampton Institute.

National Union of Teachers (2001) *Relearning to Learn: Advice to*

Teachers New to Teaching Children from Refugee and Asylum-seeking Families. London: National Union of Teachers and Department for Education.

OFSTED (2001) *Full Day Care: Guidance to the National Standards*. London: The Stationary Office.

Parten, M. (1933) Social Play Among Pre-School Children. *Journal of Abnormal and Social Psychology*, 28: 136–147.

Piaget, J. (1962) *Play, Dreams and Imitation in Childhood*. New York: Norton.

Perry, B.D. (1996) Incubated in terror: neurodevelopmental factors in the cycle of violence, in J.D. Osovsky (ed.) *Children, Youth and Violence: Searching for Solutions*. New York: Guilford Press.

Potts, S. (2003) Multi-sensory project, *Early Childhood Practice*, 5(1): 22–36.

Pynoos, R.S. and Nader, K. (1993) Issues in the treatment of post-traumatic stress in children and adolescents, in J.P. Wilson and B. Raphael (eds) *International Handbook of Traumatic Stress Syndrome*. New York: Plenum Press.

QCA (2000) *Curriculum Guidance for the Foundation Stage*. London: QCA.

Refugee Action (2003) *Is It Safe Here?* London: Refugee Action.

Refugee Council (2002) http://www.refugeecouncil.org.uk/news/myths.

Richman, N. (1996) *Principles of Help for Children Involved in Organised Violence*. London: Save the Children.

Roopnarine, J.L., Johnson, J.E. and Hooper, F. (1994) *Children's Play in Diverse Cultures*. New York: SUNY.

Rosenthal, A. and Rosanthal, S. (1980) Holocaust effect in the third generation: Child of another time. *American Journal of Psychotherapy*, 26(4) 572–880.

Rutter, J. (2001) *Supporting Refugee Children in the 21st Century: A Compendium of Essential Information*. Stoke-on-Trent: Trentham Books.

Rutter, J. and Hyder, T. (1998) *Refugee Children in the Early Years: Issues for Policy-makers and Providers*. London: Save the Children.

Rutter, M. (1981) Stress, coping and development: some lessons and some questions. *Journal of Child Psychiatry*, 22, 323–356.

Rutter, M. (1985) Resilience in the face of adversity: protective factors and resistance to psychiatric disorder, *British Journal of Psychiatry*, 147: 598–611.

Salusbury World and Save the Children (2004) *Home from Home: A Guidance and Resource Pack for the Welcome and Inclusion of Refugee Children and Families in School*. London: Salusbury World and Save the Children.

Save the Children (2003) http://www.savethechildren.org.uk/scuk/jsp/history.

Save the Children and the Refugee Council (2001) *In Safe Hands: A Resource and Training Pack to Support Work with Young Refugee Children*. London: Save the Children.

Sayeed, Z. and Guerin, E. (2000) *Early Years Play: A Happy Medium for Assessment and Intervention*. London: David Fulton.

Schiller, F. (1845) *The Aesthetic Letters, Essays and Philosophical Letters*. Boston: Little Brown.

Shore, R. (1997) *Rethinking the Brain: New Insights into Early Development*. New York: Families and Work Institute.

Sims, M. (2000) *Young children who experienced refugee or war-related trauma*, paper presented at the 10th European Early Education Childhood Education Research Association, London.

Sims, M., Hayden, J., Palmer, G. and Hutchins, T. (2002) Young children who have experienced refugee or war-related trauma, *European Early Childhood Education Research Journal*, 10(1).

Siraj- Blatchford, I. and Clarke, P. (2000) *Supporting Identity, Diversity and Language in the Early Years*. Buckingham: Open University Press.

Skinner, B. F. (1938) *The Behaviour of Organisms: An Experimental Analysis*. Cambridge MA: BF Skinner Foundation.

Spencer, H. (1878) *The Principles of Psychology*. Appleton: New York.

Terr, C. (1981) Forbidden games: post-traumatic child's play, *American Academy of Child Psychiatry*, 20(4): 741–60.

Tolfree, D. (1996) *Restoring Playfulness: Different Approaches to Assisting Children who are Psychologically Affected by War or Displacement*. Stockholm: Radda Barnen.

Trevarthen, C. (1979) Communication and Co-operation in Early Infancy: A Description of primary Intersubjectivity, Before Speech. Cambridge University Press.

United Nations (1954) *United Nations Convention Relating to the Status of Refugees* Article 1.

United Nations (1989) *United Nations Convention on the Rights of the Child (UNCRC)*. http://www.unhchr.ch/html/menu3/b/k2crc.htm.

United Nations High Commissioner for Refugees (UNHCR) (2004) http://www.unhcr.ch/statist/main.htm.

UNICEF (1993) *Children in War: A Guide to the Provision of Services*. New York: United Nations Children's Fund.

UNICEF (1996) http://www.unicef.org/graca/information

Vygotsky, L. (1978) *Mind in Society*. Cambridge MA: Harvard University Press.

Winnicott, D.W. (1971) *Playing and Reality*. London: Routledge.

INDEX

abstract thinking 16
access to early years services 36–9
'accommodation' 16
activities, play-based 85–8
adults *see* caregivers; parents;
    practitioner/therapist roles;
    teachers
age
    birth to 3 years 9, 10, 12–13, 43–4,
        70, 78
    4–6 years 93
    risk factors 54
aggressive behaviour 12, 43, 48, 49,
    50
Amnesty International 25, 51–2
anger 50–1
anxiety/fear 44, 48, 50
art therapy 20, 85–6
'assimilation' 16
Asylum and Immigration Act (1998)
    31
asylum-seekers/refugees
    application outcomes 29–34
    reasons for flight 26–8
    statistics 28, 30
    terminology 4, 24–5
    see also children; communities/
        families; early years services
auditory learners 87
Axline, V. 20

behavioural manifestations of stress
    43, 71–2, 73
behavioural norms, impact of war
    7–8
behaviourist perspective 16–17
belonging, encouraging 81
Blackwell, D. and Melzak, S. 95

blame 50–1
Bracken, P.J. 46
brain development 10–13
Brandenburger, D. 85
Bromly, H. 86
Bronfenbrenner, U. 8, 9
Brown, B. 75, 77, 86
Bruce, T. 14, 15, 16, 17–18, 21, 81,
    82

caregivers
    attention/responsiveness 12, 78,
        95
    clinging to 43
    impact of war and violence 44–5,
        48–9
    interventions in violent play 91
    relationship-building 65, 75, 82–3
    secure attachment 11, 12, 13
    training/recruitment 38–9, 76,
        96–7, 98
    see also communities/families;
        parents; practitioner/therapist
        roles
case studies 27–8, 54–5
'catharsis' 16
Cattanach, A. 21, 88
child development 5–6, 8–9
    brain 10–13
    impact of war and violence 43–4,
        45–6
    role of play 12, 13–22
child psychotherapy movement
    20
child rape 8, 52
children
    application outcomes 29–30, 31,
        32, 33–4

communication with 69–71
impact of war and violence 42–4,
45–54
National Asylum Support Service
(NASS) 31, 36
rights 3–4, 34, 36, 100–1
as victims of conflict 1–4, 25, 34–5
whole child perspective 62–4
clinging to carers 43
clinical manifestations of stress 43
cognitive development 16
and social/emotional development
19, 21–2
Cohen, D. 13, 15, 19
Cole, E.K.H. 33–4
communication
with children 69–71
with parents 65–6
about play 68
play as 70–1
'scripts' 16, 71
communities/families 31–2, 35–6
focus 54–6
healing 96–7
and identity 22, 39, 46, 83–4
impact of war and violence 6–8
working with 95–7
competence 45
conflict, terminology 4
coping strategies 7–8, 45, 50, 54–6, 57
counselling 66, 96
cultural contexts/differences 42, 71–2
education 39
play 21–2, 37, 65, 68–9, 81
see also identity
curriculum, play-based 68–9, 78–9,
97–8

dance 83–4, 85
Daycare Trust 38, 71–2
Declaration of the Rights of the Child 3
definitions/terminology 4, 14–15,
24–5, 41
Department for Education and Skills
(DfES) 78, 98
depression
childhood 48, 50
parental 11, 66

Derman-Sparks, L. 75
detention of asylum-seekers 32–4
'discretionary leave' 29
discrimination *see* racism
dispersal policy 31–2
dreams 42, 47–8
dressing-up clothes 85, 87

Early Years Development and
Childcare Partnerships 38
early years services 60–76
access 36–9
uptake 97–8
'ecological development' 8, 9
Edenhammer, K. and Wahlund, C. 71
education
cultural context 39
loss of 52
right to 34, 36
see also early years services;
practitioner/therapist roles;
teachers
Elbedour, S. *et al.* 41, 44, 54, 55–6
emotional development 19, 21–2
emotional expression 70
emotional support 66–8, 71–3
endocrine/limbic system
development 11
English language 37, 58, 66
acquisition 82, 91–2
women 36, 38
exceptional leave to remain (ELR) 29,
30
excess energy 15–16
eye contact 71

families *see* communities/families
fear/anxiety 44, 48, 50
free-flow play 18–19, 82
see also imaginative/make-believe
play
Freud, A. 19–20, 56, 57
and Burlingham, D. 49
Freud, S. 16

gender
girls 32, 34, 52
risk factors 54

violent play 90, 91, 92, 93
women 8, 34, 35–6, 38
good practice frameworks
  61–2
Gopnik, A. *et al.* 5, 10, 11, 78
gun play 90–3

healing
  communities 96–7
  and play 18–21, 42, 56–7, 61
historical perspectives
  play theories 13–14, 15–19
  refugees 24–6
Holland, P. 91–2, 93
home corners 84–5
Home Office, UK 28, 29, 30,
  32–3
Hourani *et al.* 51
Huizinga, J. 13–14
'humanitarian protection' 29
Hutt, C. 17–18
Hyder, T. 49, 60, 73, 85
  Rutter, J. and 37, 82
Hyun, E. 21–2

identifying with aggressors
  50–1
identity 22, 39, 46, 83–4
imaginative/make-believe play 12,
  17, 18
  see also free-flow play
increased arousal 48
indefinite leave to remain (ILR)
  29
individual sessions 73
induction/settling in 80–1
information 79–80
  lack of 37
  sources 80–1
instinctual urges 16
intergenerational affects of trauma
  55–6
Isaacs, S. 19

Jebb, E. 2–3

key-worker system 82–3
kinaesthetic learners 87–8

Klein, M. 19–20
Krogh , Y. and Montgomery, E. 50

Landers, C. 43, 44, 47, 48, 66, 70,
  90
landmines 25, 52
Lane, J. 74, 75, 84
language
  assessment 72
  development 70
  home 81–2, 83
  information 80
  see also English language
learning styles 87–8
limbic/endocrine system
  development 11
listening skills 70–1, 88
lone parents 35–6

Machel, G. 24–5, 100
mask-making 85–6
materials/resources 65, 84–5
Melzak, S. 51, 55, 58, 100
memory of traumatic events 48–9,
  51
Mental Health Foundation 63–4
mental representation 17
'metacommunication skills' 16
Molteno, M. 9, 65
multi-agency working 72–3
multi-sensory play 87–8
Munro, Dr. Henry 2
music 83–4, 85, 87
Mutesi, L. 66–8

National Asylum Support Service
  (NASS) 31, 36
nature vs. nurture debate 9
needs 64–5
  vs. rights 3
negative feelings about difference
  84
neural/synaptic activity 10–11
news media representations
  of asylum-seekers/refugees 30, 35,
    95, 96
  of violence 93–5
numbing of responsiveness 48

parents
  attitudes to physical punishment
    91
  communication with 65–6
  depression 11, 66
  lone 35–6
  and promotion of play 62, 67, 68,
    81, 97
  relationship with child 48–9, 50–1,
    66, 83
  torture of 27, 28, 50
  see also caregivers
Parten, M. 17
peek-a-boo 71
peers 82, 91–2
persona dolls 86
physical consequences of war on
    children 51–2, 53–4
Piaget, J. 16
play
  cultural context 21–2, 37, 65, 68–9,
    81
  definitions 14–15
  first principles 61, 64–5
  lack of access 32, 33, 34, 36–9
  right to 4, 34, 100–1
  role of 12, 13–22
  stages 20–1
  taxonomies 17–18
play frames 88
play-based activities 85–8
play-based curriculum 68–9, 78–9,
    97–8
popular culture 91
post-traumatic stress disorder (PTSD)
    46, 56
  see also stress; trauma
Potts, S. 87–8
practitioner/therapist roles 78–9, 93
  communication 65–71
  referral 71–3
  stuckness 57–8
  supportive 64, 75–6
  working with communities/
    families 95–7
  see also caregivers; teachers
protective factors 63, 64
protective play 20

psychoanalytical perspectives 16,
    18–21, 56–7, 96
psychosocial stress 52, 53
Pynoos, R.S. and Nader, K. 47, 49, 53,
    56, 57

racism 36, 38
  tackling discrimination 73–5
re-experiencing trauma 47–8
'recapitulation theory' 16
recovery
  factors 52–3
  through play 54–6, 57
'recreational'/'relaxation' theory
    15–16
recruitment/training 38–9, 76, 96–7,
    98
referrals 71–3
Refugee Action 36
Refugee Council 26, 28, 29, 31, 37,
    80–1
  as information source 80–1
refugees
  definition 25
  see also asylum-seekers/refugees
relationships
  peers 82, 91–2
  practitioner/therapist role 21, 58
  trust 45, 62
  see also caregivers; parents
repetitive play 16, 47, 48
  stuckness 57–8, 97
research literature 49–51
resolution *see* recovery
resources/materials 65, 84–5
responsibility for events, sense of 44,
    51
responsiveness
  caregivers 12, 78, 95
  numbing of 48
Richman, N. 46–7, 73
rights 3–4, 34, 36, 100–1
  vs. needs 3
risk factors 63–4
role-play 85–6
Roopnarine, J.L. *et al.* 21, 22, 68
Rousseau, J. J. 14
routines, building upon 75

Rutter, J. and Hyder, T. 37, 82
Rutter, M. 54, 62, 63–4
  Hyder, T. and 37

safety/security 9
  in relationships 11, 12, 13, 65, 75,
    82–3
  threats to 53–4
Salusbury World refugee project 28,
  32
Save the Children 3, 32, 34, 37, 49
  founding 2–3
  Sweden 61
schooling *see* education
'scripts' 16, 71
self, sense of *see* identity
self-esteem building 74, 76
self-initiation 15
sensory play 20
sexual violence 34, 36
  child rape 8, 52
Shore, R. 10, 11, 12
Sims, M. 69, 83
  et al. 76, 91
Siraj-Blatchford, I. and Clarke, P. 74
Skinner, B.F. 16
social development 16, 19, 21–2,
  55
social networks *see* communities/
  families
social norms, impact of war 7–8
space 64–5
  and structure, STOP framework
    61–2
special educational needs services 72,
  98
Spencer, H. 15
spiritual manifestations of stress 43
spontaneity 15
stages in therapeutic play 20–1
STOP framework 61–2
storyboxes 86–7
stress
  child development perspective
    11–12, 43–4, 45–6
  coping strategies 7–8, 45, 50, 54–6,
    57
  cultural context 42

manifestations 43, 71–2, 73
  post-traumatic stress disorder
    (PTSD) 46, 56
  psychosocial 52, 53
  see also trauma
stuckness 57–8, 97
superhero play 91–2, 93
Sure Start 38, 98
surplus energy 15–16
symbolic play 16–17, 20, 47, 71
synaptic/neural activity 10–11

talking 62
taxonomies of play 17–18
teachers 67
  status 39
  see also practitioner/therapist roles
television *see* news media; popular
  culture
terminology/definitions 4, 14–15,
  24–5, 41
therapists *see* practitioner/therapist
  roles
time, STOP framework 62
Tolfree, D. 61, 64, 96
torture, parental 27, 28, 50
toys 65, 83
  weapons 90–3
training/recruitment 38–9, 76, 96–7,
  98
trauma
  concept of 46–7
  and play 47–8
  'traumatic avoidance' 56–7
  see also stress
trust 45, 62
turn-taking 71

UNICEF 42, 43, 51, 52, 53, 54
United Nations Convention on Refugees
  25, 29
United Nations Convention on the
  Rights of the Child (UNCRC) 3–4,
  34
United Nations High Commission for
  Refugees (UNHCR) 24

victimhood, sense of 54

SUPPORTING INCLUSION IN THE EARLY YEARS

Caroline A. Jones

- What is inclusive education and how can it be developed in early childhood?

This accessible book provides guidance on the inclusion of young children with special educational needs or disabilities in early education settings. The emphasis is on inclusion as a process aimed at supporting young children and their families. The author highlights the complexity of early identification and assessment of children described as having special educational needs, and encourages readers to consider important questions relating to the language and values underpinning early years policy and practice. The theoretical perspectives are supported by examples based on concerns and experiences of parents, children and practitioners.

- Examines the ways in which children with special educational needs and/or disabilities are identified, assessed and supported
- Highlights the importance of working with parents and colleagues to enable children's individual needs to be met
- Promotes the development of an early years culture where inclusion of all children is regarded as a right rather than an option
- Encompasses a variety of early education settings, for example playgroups, nurseries and the early years of primary school

Supporting Inclusion in the Early Years has implications for the teaching and learning of all young children, not only those perceived as having special educational needs. It is essential reading for anyone working or intending to work with young children.

Contents
Acknowledgements – Introduction – Labels, language and inclusion – Early identification and assessment – A graduated model of assessment and provision – The changing role of the Special Educational Needs Co-ordinator (SENCO) – Developing inclusive policy and practice – Parents, children and professionals working together – Beyond the Paintpots : Inclusion and Learning Support Assistants – Useful addresses – References

144pp   0 335 21091 0 (Paperback)   0 335 21092 9 (Hardback)

StEPS: STATEMENTS OF ENTITLEMENT TO PLAY
A FRAMEWORK FOR PLAYFUL TEACHING

Janet Moyles and Sian Adams

The basis of this video and book pack is a belief in the rights of the young child to appropriate opportunities to be children and to learn in playful and meaningful ways. It is also predicated upon a view that practitioners working with young children have equal rights to teach using playful strategies.

Children and adults are responsible for making the most of the playful learning and teaching opportunities provided in quality early childhood settings and to ensure that the curriculum – statutory or recommended – is implemented efficiently and effectively. The view taken throughout is that there is no conflict between being accountable to parents, politicians or providers for children's learning and offering play experiences as the basis for that learning.

Playful teaching and learning are discussed and exemplified throughout the two elements of the Pack. The video offers viewers a chance to see some of the practitioners who contributed to the Pack, in their own settings using aspects of StEPs to support their everyday teaching and learning. One of the major intentions of the Pack is that it should be used by practitioners and settings – or those undertaking training sessions with them – to both evaluate and extend play practices. The video, child development charts, planning sheets and other documentation, explained in various sections, support a variety of uses across a range of settings reflecting different backgrounds and ethos. Once the framework is understood, the StEPs themselves offer endless opportunities for development of quality learning experiences for children and for articulation, explanation and advocacy of quality practice by practitioners to parents, inspectors and those who evaluate settings.

112pp   0 335 20717 0 Training Pack
The video cassette in this pack is designed for PAL systems.

UNDERSTANDING EARLY CHILDHOOD

Helen Penn

Understanding Early Childhood offers a broad and wide-ranging perspective on the ways in which we try to understand young children. It summarizes some of the current debates in child development and looks at other forms of understanding and the kinds of methods used to gain understanding. It explores personal memories of childhood; neuro-scientific and genetic interpretations of childhood; and cultural understandings. Drawing on research evidence from across the world, it includes chapters on history, health and child rights. The book concludes with an analysis of everyday practices in working with young children from across the world.

This book is key reading for early childhood students and practitioners.

Contents
Preface – Remembering Childhood – Researching Reality – Not Piaget Again – Genes, Neurons and Ancestors – The Other Side of the World – Past Present and Future – Children's Rights: A New Approach to Studying Childhood – Hoping for Health – Practice Makes No Difference – References

Contributors
Priscilla Alderson; Val Thurtle

c.192pp   0 335 21134 8 (Paperback)   0 335 21135 6 (Hardback)

Related books from Open University Press
Purchase from www.openup.co.uk or order through your
local bookseller

Education in an Urbanised Society
Series Editors: Gerald Grace, Meg Maguire & Ian Menter

REFUGEE CHILDREN IN THE UK

Jill Rutter

The issue of asylum seekers and refugees causes intense media and political debate. Whilst the political debate centres on entry control, much
of the media coverage is negative. However, little attention has been
paid to how asylum seekers and refugees could be helped to rebuild their
lives in the UK or elsewhere. This book analyses the social policies that
impact on refugee children's education and features:

- An informative background to the migration of refugees
- An outline of international refugee law
- How policy towards refugees is made
- How policy relates to practice
- Current issues of concern
- Case studies examining refugee children's experiences
- Alternative visions for refugee settlement

Drawing on the testimonies of refugee children, this timely book brings
a much-needed insight into the pressing problems and needs of refugee
children. It is valuable reading for students of education, sociology and
social policy as well as education, health and social work professionals.

Contents

*Part One: Introduction – Introduction – Global overview – Part Two: Refugee
Policy – Refugee settlement in the UK: history repeats itself – The creation of
non-citizens: today's asylum policy – The integration agenda – The influence
of Europe – Researching refugees – Part Three: Refugee Children – The under
fives – The education of asylum-seeking and refugee children: policy – The
education of asylum-seeking and refugee children: unresolved issues –
Unaccompanied children – Healthcare – Alternative visions.*

c.160pp   0 335 21373 1 (Paperback)   0 335 21374 X (Hardback)

violence
  in play 90–3
  terminology 4
  see also sexual violence; war
Vygotsky, L. 17

war
  impact on carers 44–5, 48–9
  impact on children 42–4,
    45–54
  impact on communities 6–8

terminology 4, 41
  see also violence
weapons 24–5
  toy 90–3
whole child perspective 62–4
Winnicott, D.W. 20
withdrawn behaviour 69
women 8, 34, 35–6, 38

'zero tolerance' approach to violent
  play 91, 92, 93